AF437143

All The Pretty Houses

Harmonie Lovin

First published in the United States of America by What's Next? Publishing.
Copyright © 2023 by Harmonie Lovin
All rights reserved. No part of this publication may be reproduced, stored, or transmitted in any form or by any means, electronic, mechanical, photocopying, recording, scanning, or otherwise without written permission from the publisher. It is illegal to copy this book, post it to a website, or distribute it by any other means without permission. Harmonie Lovin asserts the moral right to be identified as the author of this work.

Cover Design by Jason Arias

Harmonie Lovin has no responsibility for the persistence or accuracy of URLs for external or third-party Internet Websites referred to in this publication and does not guarantee that any content on such Websites is, or will remain, accurate or appropriate. Designations used by companies to distinguish their products are often claimed as trademarks. All brand names and product names used in this book and on its cover are trade names, service marks, trademarks, and registered trademarks of their respective owners. The publishers and the book are not associated with any product or vendor mentioned in this book. None of the companies referenced within the book have endorsed the book.

Some names and identifying details have been changed in order to protect individual privacy. There are 3 sides to any event: theirs, mine, and the truth. Any recreation of people, places, or conversations are only accurate in my memory.

First edition U.S. Paperback Printing: August 2023

979-8-9885537-0-0

Acknowledgments

Mr. Anderson (my ninth-grade English teacher) taught me to never fall in love with my first draft. Thanks for the advice.

Many thanks to my family for supporting me through this process, who gave me pause to think and forever changed my perspective on love, kindness, and forgiveness, and who put up with me asking them to read random chapters. You were there for me on the hardest day of my life, and I owe you my deepest gratitude.

Special thanks to my husband, CJ, for loving me through the last decade and allowing me to cry as I revisited my past.

David, thanks for choosing to be my dad. Without you in my life, I'm not sure who I'd be today, but you certainly played a large part in who I became.

I must acknowledge my editor, Michael McConnell. Thank you for your patience, your feedback, and expertise.

For my son.

I love you more than anything in the universe, the galaxy, or the stars in the sky.

Hiraeth *n.* (Welsh) A spiritual longing for a home which maybe never was. Nostalgia for ancient places to which we cannot return. It is the echo for the lost places of our soul's past and our grief for them. It is in the wind and the rocks and the waves. It is nowhere and it is everywhere.

Introduction

People often ask where I'm from, as I have no distinct accent or strikingly unusual appearance. It's a friendly question, one that often isn't intended as anything more than an ice-breaker. Sometimes I state my birthplace, while other times I simply say my current town. I'm well practiced at the answer. I'm also well practiced at how to avoid it. Typically, most military children move six to nine times during their school years. If only I had been *that* lucky! *My parents were on the lam.* Even as I type this, I can't hide my laughter. It's far from true, but admittedly, it's my favorite answer.

Sometimes, on rare occasions, I tell the truth. I've lived in twelve states. Then the genuine intrigue comes pouring out, and the questions that I know will follow. "What state did you like the best?" "What was your favorite house?" "Why did you move so much?"

Some answers are easy. I loved South Dakota more than any other state I've lived in. Of the more than forty houses I can remember, my favorite was probably the one in Idaho. That last answer, though, is far more complicated and takes much longer to explain, but I'm finally ready to tell you.

All the days I've lived (and the memories that have been cultivated of those days) have brought me here. The story I tell is part of me. It's ugly and beautiful. It's a mixture of loss and grief, triumphs and perseverance. I don't believe my life is extraordinary, but instead very ordinary. Shared experiences are rarely remembered consistently, and all of the details are seldom the same. These stories are my memories and my lessons from my journey here on Earth.

What do you remember? Memory can be a fickle friend. At times, it can take us to a place or a moment we had forgotten long ago, or so it seemed. Yet more times than I can count, I've gone in search of an item left in another room, picturing exactly where it is, like my freshly brewed coffee I left in the kitchen. I go to retrieve it, only to enter the room, glancing from wall to wall, and wonder, "What the hell did I come in here for!"

If I'm lucky enough to spy the swirly gray mug resting on the edge of the counter, I will have victory! Other times I admit defeat and walk out, only to remember it again! I'm not losing my mind or my memory. This is a phenomenon called the "doorway effect." It happens because we have changed our environment and we become more consumed with the here and now and the new room we've entered than the reason we entered it.

Alternatively, I've walked into a house I've never been to before and suddenly remembered something from my past. It's like a TV channel suddenly flips on and a segment of my life flashes in my mind. The science behind it explains it as our mind recognizing a current thought or feeling that's parallel with a moment from the past.

I'm most fond of "mind-pops," a term coined in 1997 that refers to memories unexpectedly recalled from one's past. It's not a memory you chose to think of. It may be good or bad, but all of a sudden it's there for no apparent reason. Those fleeting memories, I say, are when I forget to remember. I think memories make up 99 percent of us. The 1 percent left is the present moment that, if you allow it to pass, will soon become a memory as well.

Of all our senses, the one with the strongest link to memory is smell. It can easily propel you back to a former lover, the high school locker room where you celebrated your first win, the hospital where your grandfather died, or something altogether insignificant. I love the smell of hot chocolate and warm, buttered toast. My mother would often prepare the treat for me as a child on cold winter days. Now, as soon as I bite into the warmth of the butter, drenched in the sweetness of the decadent chocolate, I'm instantly taken back there. It's my comfort food and tastes like love to me, still, all these years later.

I feel as though I have been crafting the words upon these pages my entire life. Just under the surface of every moment and every memory, a piece of me has seeded and grown. Every place I've touched has, in turn, touched me. Each chapter of my life has told a story, and inside each one a part of me still exists.

As I sit on the oversize couch, with the down feather pillows allowing me to balance the laptop on my knees, the black keys beckon me to strike their letters. Yet, I find myself reflecting on the changes this house has endured. The bland yellow that adorned the tattered walls when I first stepped through the front door is now comforted in an earthy green, bringing new life. The cold blue of the master bedroom that illuminated sadness was the first to go, painted over in a fresh gray, along with crisp white baseboards.

I run my feet over the luscious rug that magnifies the original hardwood floors and wonder how many feet have walked these wooden planks. From visitors and family to creatures with four paws or little toes, the stomps of teens and the weary steps of the old. How many lives had this house known before I claimed it as my own? Had it been here waiting for me all along? If the house had memories, what would they be and what secrets would it try to confess? The house would never tell, and the creak of the floorboards and shifts inside the earth almost dare me to unveil them.

I gaze through the bay windows that look out into the well-manicured neighborhood. The little houses built in the fifties line together as they stretch down and around the circle at the end, then up again, creating an imaginary question mark. The bright beams of sun illuminate the snow that covers the rooftops and I'm slightly blinded by its glare. My eyes fall upon the large oaks with barren winter leaves and the pines in the distance. Suddenly, I'm struck with a memory I hadn't thought of in so long, I'd almost forgotten it altogether.

I'm sitting in the back of the old silver car, gazing out the window. My mom is at the wheel, her blond hair happily dancing in the warmth of the summer air. There isn't a destination, only a long drive down the backroads that provides cheap entertainment in the midst of a long hot summer. The old, tattered houses and fields surrounding them, full of black and brown cows, pass before me. I look out upon the green pastures and admire the horses as their tails sway with unabashed freedom in the subtle breeze of the midafternoon.

I stretch my small arm out the window and fan the wind. Its force pushes my hand back and up and down and forward. The rays of light shine down on my face and warm me with happiness that can only be experienced in the summer sun.

But when the car changes direction, with scenery I don't recognize, my stomach becomes unsettled. The warmth I felt is replaced with a chill from the shadows of the tall pines that loom over me. As I look down the unfamiliar road, I ask my mother, "Are we lost?" As always, she replies with the same answer. "We're not lost. We're just

going down the road a piece." Down the road a piece.

10

The First

I was born on a cold winter's day in Wisconsin.

Before my first birthday we'd already moved on to

Oklahoma. Just one year after that, we found

ourselves in a new home, where the blazing sun

scorched the grass and the days passed slowly, as

though time was also too hot to tick by any faster.

My mom had just entered her early thirties and

returned to her demanding career as a homemaker

and mother of four. Although she'd closed her

shortlived interior decorating business, it did

nothing to curb her keen eye for detail. She spilled

her talents into every corner of the house, including

my and my sister's room. It was painted in a pale

pink with a homemade white picket fence that

outlined our play area. It was perfect for her two daughters and everything two little girls could want: full of toys placed neatly on shelves and the laughter of two sisters that were happy to have one another.

My earliest memory is sitting on a bench waiting for my turn to jump rope. I distinctly recall watching the rope looping up and down in the empty garage of my sister's playmate's house. Suddenly I felt something warm and hot. As I reached down to investigate my calf, I was struck with a sudden and horrible pain. I had just been stung by a scorpion! I screamed out and began to cry. My sister immediately threw down the rope and rushed over to me.

April was a petite child with small features and long auburn hair and little more than four years my elder. She heaved me into her arms and bravely trotted across the street, back to our house and into my mother's care. I lay on the couch as my dad scooped up a ball of tobacco and shoved it in his cheek. The pain seared up my thigh, and I looked up at him in search of rescue. He stuck his fingers in his mouth and pulled out the black goo, slapping the bitter wad onto my leg in hopes that it would draw out the sting. Sitting beside me, he spooned sweet vanilla ice cream into my mouth until my tears had been quenched. By the time the bowl was empty, the sting had subsided.

There aren't many memories of the first house. I sort of recall my pet rock, Herman. He was gray and oval shaped, with fine white lines that ran along his smooth surface. I partially remember my and April's bedroom. But I definitely remember the Texan heat and the sting from the scorpion. Otherwise there's no indication of much else, just photos of my parents donning cowboy hats next to the red brick fireplace.

It's said that negative memories are much easier to recall. *Is it* much easier to remember the sting of the scorpion than the pink room full of innocent laughter? Perhaps the memories contain the lessons that created the person I was to become. Had I remembered further back, my story may have been different. I may have been different.

I don't remember much about Texas. I don't remember much . . . until Colorado. Colorado is where it all started. Where I began to become me, and my family went from *us* to *them*. It's where I can recount the beginning of the end, although I wasn't able to see it then.

The House in the Mountains

The three-story split level had two staircases from the main floor. One running up and the other leading down. The bay windows faced the quaint street and framed the magnificent mountaintops dusted in white powder. It was also where our cat, Muffy, would chase the birds who antagonized her from the sill. It was the second house we occupied in Colorado, moving from Colorado Spring to Fort Collins in just under a year.

Despite having April and another older brother, I thought no one was better than Bryan! Bryan was a talented artist, and during our time in Colorado, his work was entered into a state contest. He won by a landslide, and his pieces received the honor of being showcased at the art museum in the city. By far, art was what he loved the most. It was typical to find him in front of a canvas, his hands saturated with colorful oils and a brush tucked behind his ear, as he worked on his latest masterpiece.

There were ten years between Bryan and me. As the oldest, he was often in charge of tending to his siblings. As the youngest, I didn't take very kindly to being bossed around. I'd warn him that when I got older than him, I would get to tell *him* what to do! Clearly, I didn't understand the concept of how ages worked. I also expected to eventually be taller than him. Bryan was easily six feet tall at fourteen and would happily oblige when I requested that he "dodo me." He'd pick me up and lift me into the air, touching my head on the ceiling and then quickly set me back down to the floor, resulting in my stomach flip-flopping.

Although Bryan had two other siblings, every afternoon he'd walk home from school and eat lunch with me. The meal was always a choice between ramen soup or oatmeal. He liked to trick me by saying, "Hey, did you see that bird over there?" I would look and he'd take a bite of my lunch or steal the last French fry at dinner. Eventually I caught on, but sometimes I'd turn and look, just to let him know that the game was still on.

My mother was notorious for taking in strays, so one day when Bryan brought home a lively golden retriever, she allowed him to keep it, with the understanding that the puppy was restricted to the downstairs. Bryan was diligent about tending to the dog's business and he happily showed off the new pup at the park and everywhere else he went. Bryan named him Jessie. The dog may have been the only thing Bryan loved more than his art.

Then one day when my siblings were off at school, Jessie whined at me from the bottom of the stairs. While my mother busied herself in the kitchen, I quietly sneaked down the steps until I was standing in front of the wooden plank that held the pup on the other side. Jessie licked my hand, but I couldn't quite reach him, so I decided to remove the barrier and give him a closer pet. Just as I lifted it up, he bolted past me and charged up the stairs, straight after Muffy! My mom yelled out at the theatrics of a puppy ready for a chase. She scooped up Muffy and returned Jessie to the downstairs doggie jail. I begged her to let me play with him, but he was Bryan's dog, and I would have to wait until my brother returned from school.

So, I snatched Muffy from her perch on the alcove. I pulled out my best doll clothes and pushed her fuzzy arms through the openings. Minutes later, Muffy sauntered down the stairs while I proudly yelled out for my mom to take a look. I couldn't wait to try out the clothes on Jessie, but not long afterward my dad left with her. Bryan was devastated when he returned from school to find that his best friend had

been given away without a chance to say goodbye.

That night I stood at the bottom of the staircase,

bewildered by the shouts and the sight of an

argument that had taken place at its crest. My father

pointed downward and referred to Jessie as "that

damn dog." My mom raised her voice, asking how he

could be so cold. Out of nowhere, Bryan turned the

corner and shoved me out of the way. I heard a

rumble as though thunder was tumbling down the

stairs and then I heard my mother cry.

We sat quietly in the waiting room at the hospital.

Every so often, I'd look over at Bryan. His bifocals

hid any expression that may have been revealed in

his eyes. He had sheltered me from the violent act

yet forced himself to endure the pain. Through the

years, I'd come to know him as the protector of the

family, until he passed the proverbial baton to me before I ever knew how badly I would need it.

Days later I sat beside my mother on the plane, running my fingers down the hard cast and taking note of her red nail polish. My innocence prevented me from understanding why we were taking the trip, but my mom explained we were going to visit Grandma.

Grandma was a round woman and mother of seven, with my mother being the eldest. Her big black glasses, a style left over from the 1960s, highlighted the expression lines just above the brim of her nose. Although she appeared to be a no-nonsense woman, she had a knack for making my mom laugh. Even over the phone line, I'd hear my mom roaring with laughter as I'd lie in bed. Her voice would burst through the darkness and tickle my ears, making me smile, all the while oblivious to the subject that was so funny.

Grandma was unlike her mother, my greatgrandmother, who was a soft-spoken woman. Her Midwestern accent hid her Lithuanian heritage. She'd speak to me in many languages as she held my hand in hers. There may have been no one as kind as her, and despite her bedridden state from the cancer that consumed every cell of her body, she always made time for her youngest granddaughter. Even all these years later, the thought of her is still a comfort. I'd later attend her funeral, where she lay in an open casket, looking at peace but not quite herself.

I remember standing on the wooden stool provided, so that I could say my goodbyes and then move along for others to pay their respects. I stared down at my great-grandmother's soft hands that once held mine.

It was my first experience with death or loss of any kind. So, not knowing the protocol for funeral visitation, I reached in and touched her hand once more and said aloud, "She's so cold." I remember looking up at my parents, who had begun to cry. It was a stark contrast to my grandma's funeral, where I quickly viewed her and moved aside while hiding the growing bump under my black dress. I recall thinking of the circle of life and its irony. One life had ended, making room for a new life to begin.

Although I can't recall the visit to Grandma's, I can remember, in very vivid detail, the plane. My mom ordered a drink for me, and the flight attendant gingerly set it down on the foldout tray. Then my mother blatantly told the flight attendant off and informed her that the drink was much too large for her small child. She rhetorically asked what she thought of a little girl trying to lift a cup that was bigger than both of her hands. The flight attendant smiled at me and obediently removed the large beverage from the tray and corrected her now obvious mistake, with an appropriately sized milk.

My mom's concern for an enormous milk largely overshadowed the fact that, for the first time, she'd escaped my father. The visit was brought to an abrupt end when my father told her in no uncertain terms exactly what he would do to the remaining children who were left behind if she did not return immediately with me in tow. So, we climbed in the cab of my uncle's semi and made the long journey back to the house in Colorado.

24

The Realization

Our family room often flooded. My dad would be there with mops and buckets, diligently sopping up the murky water and ringing it out with the metal pull handle. I remember trudging through the nearly waist-high water, against my father's wishes, to retrieve my beloved giant blue teddy bear. Bryan's room was also on the lower level, along with our big red couch that rounded out in a semicircle. It was a piece of furniture left over from the seventies suite that had mostly been abandoned for a newer, modern collection. Still, it was perfect for us kids since we didn't need to be concerned about damaging it as we romped and played.

Sometimes my dad would bring home refrigerator boxes and set them up in the family room. He'd carve out doors and little windows for us. After his knife work was complete, April and I would spend days with crayons, coloring the outside with bright shades and designs before it was perfectly decorated. Then our pretend land would play out through various scenarios, such as a drive-thru restaurant or an ice cream shoppe. Through the mailbox cutout, we slipped secret notes to one another addressed to "Bluebird" or "Firebird," our Native American names bestowed to us by our great-grandfather, who was Pottawatomie Indian.

Once the addition of a new gaming system called Atari arrived, even my parents found themselves taking up residence in the family room from time to time. In those moments, they played as though they'd been childhood friends, and by most standards, they had been. My mother married at sixteen to the older man, who hadn't quite matured, but at twenty-two seemed like an adult. They

competed for the high score on the game *Breakout*.

My mom became quite good at it! I'd watch the

screen as the line would move back and forth and

the little white ball would bounce up to the wall at

the top and break through a piece. I'd look over to

see my mom on the edge of her seat, gliding the

controller with an intense, furrowed brow.

Meanwhile, the four of us kids would fight over

which game to play. I always preferred *Pac-Man*,

while my brothers immersed themselves with

Asteroids.

While the red couch sat downstairs covered with old

stains and likely popcorn in between the cushions,

the new furniture was upstairs in the living room.

Silky white material covered it from top to bottom,

feeling as though it was too luxurious for our simple

middle-class home. I can't recount how many hours I

spent on that couch running my hand back and forth, watching the color turn from light white to dark. The room itself was light and airy, with subtle off-white curtains and embroidered black butterflies that draped down from the high ceiling. The butterflies were my first inspiration.

One afternoon, I demanded that my mom and dad sit on the couch and give me their full attention. I grabbed the metal baton with the white rubber ends that was once my mother's when she'd been a majorette as a teen. I turned it vertically to create a make-shift microphone and stared off at the butterflies. As I sang into the baton, I imagined I was performing at a concert. I made up the words on a whim, and my parents rewarded me with smiles and applause. It was my first performance, and although I was far too young to decide what my future would be, I was positive that music would be a large part of

it.

On the top floor, there were three bedrooms. April

and I shared one. My mom built tall wooden shelves

and, at our request, painted each with our favorite

Care Bear. She meticulously drew out white puffy

clouds on the walls and painted the room a light

blue. She loved drawing intricate scenes, and she

wasn't just good at it, she was fantastic! I'm not sure

that she ever quite appreciated her own talent, but

there were few houses where she didn't leave her

mark on a wall.

My mom also drew an intricate tiger in my other

brother's room. It spoke volumes about him that he

had chosen this particular animal. Dan was

squished in the middle between Bryan and April. He

was the funniest out of us four. He didn't have the art

talent of my mom and Bryan, but what he lacked in

drawing he made up for in music, impressions, and comedy.

I remember Dan playing guitar for the first time. Bryan summoned all of us to the family room and flipped on the radio. "Stairway to Heaven" played out of the small speakers, and for a moment, we stood there, unamused. Then, as Dan listened and strummed his guitar for a moment, he started playing the song. The chords and riffs matched perfectly with Jimmy Page as though they'd been rehearsing together for decades. That's when we realized he could play by ear.

Dan would go through an almost nightly entertainment set while we all waited for dinner to be ready. He'd start out with some breakdancing, followed by the latest jokes he'd memorized. Then Dan would laugh at himself as he impersonated Eddie Murphy's laugh. It sounded as though the man himself were standing right next to you. Then we would all crack up in hilarious laughter.

His list of talents also included ventriloquism, and on one exceptionally grand Christmas, he received a dummy. It wasn't long before he became quite good and added it to his repertoire. The dummy became his prized possession, and so I was surprised to see it mutilated on the floor of his bedroom and the tiger scratched with angry pencil slashes the day Dan disappeared. Although I was too naive to understand how a young boy could run away from his family, I did not need to question why.

The house was lively and wild, perhaps a prelude of what was to come. Meanwhile, I began half days at kindergarten and met new friends, but my siblings were still my first pick as playmates. I adored each of them and wanted to be a part of their bonds that had been formed before I came along. There's nothing quite like sibling rivalry to solidify your place in the family, and I worked diligently at finding mine.

I'd been captivated when I watched Dan put together his racecar track and asked if I could play. I was told it was for boys only, intriguing me even more. He and Bryan would push the orange triggers down, and their cars would zoom around the track. I watched with excitement and yearning. I was never given a turn, and so when they went off to school, I'd sneak over to the track and hold both controllers in my hands and pretend that I was the driver. I raced around each loop and turn, before carefully placing the cars back where I found them.

Afterward, I'd return to the room I shared with April and search under her bed and around her pillows until I found the plastic pink box. I'd pull out the cartridges and place a piece of fresh white paper on top and thoughtfully choose a crayon color. Purple

was my favorite, and I thought the etching that

created the outline of the woman and her dress,

looked the most beautiful in that shade. When my

siblings returned home, they would call out to my

mom with anger upon realizing I had played with

their things again. They would beg her to stop me.

But what had they expected from their little sister,

who just wanted to be a part of their club?

Finally, I relented and abandoned their toys when

my parents returned home one day with a playful

cocker spaniel named Mickey. He quickly became

my best friend. I taught him to sit and even to pull

my little toy telephone. He'd prance through the

house, and you'd hear the bells of the phone not far

behind him. For bedtime, I'd religiously brush his

teeth while he lapped up the minty cream. He

brought a blissful innocence and new joy to the

house, masking any notion that we were anything other than a typical middle-class family.

Yet, the normalcy of those moments hadn't washed away the memories of the past. Those years, the abuse of my mother was not outright. We knew, but we didn't. Bryan had witnessed the broken arm in Colorado when my father had pushed my mother down the stairs, but in Indiana there was silence between them. A calm before the storm.

Of course, there were those nights I'd hear my mom watching TV alone. Sometimes, I'd sit at the top of the stairs, unable to find the courage to announce that I couldn't sleep. My mom would often catch me and offer a bowl of cereal before sending me back to my room, while other times she would scream for me to "Go!" I'd run, stumbling up the stairs until I reached the safety of my bed.

If my dad wasn't absent, he was cruel and made it known that 2x4s were not just for building. If my brothers were in trouble, we knew what the punishment would be. I remember nightmares, fueled by my dad's sadistic idea of entertainment. He would paint his face in scary makeup and run into our room after we settled down to sleep. We would cry in horror as he stood over us laughing until his face turned as red as his hair. In the dawn hours, my dreams would frighten me awake, and I'd run to my parents' locked bedroom door and lie outside on the floor as tears streamed down my face. Then I'd see feet coming toward me and the hem of my sister's long green nightgown. She'd take my hand and lead me back to her bed for comfort.

April and I often shared a bed and, just as often, got scolded due to our giggles. She would take my long blond locks and pretend to eat my "spaghetti hair." I was highly ticklish, and she loved making me squeal, leaving me flailing all over the bed and keeping my siblings awake with laughter. Even my mother at times amused herself as she softly powered my hand and told me to concentrate while she tickled my palm.

The days were dusted with moments of humor and love and so I became condition to be prepared for the unexpected. It was implausible to know what could happen next, not because I was so young, but because you just cannot know what you cannot imagine. Later, I'd recognize the parallel of my childhood and motherhood with startling clarity. While one night giggles bounced through the walls, the next day may have been phrenetic. Much like the day that had been nothing short of ordinary until my dad collected our three hamsters from their living quarters. Holding them in his tight fists, my dad walked into the bathroom. April and I looked at him with inquisitive eyes, though we were not prepared for the horror that was about to take place. One hamster plopped into the toilet. I stood there staring as my sister's hamster clawed its way from the maelstrom of the toilet bowl, only to be sucked down anyways. Then the next hamster met the same fate and the last. Flush after flush. My father showed no remorse or joy at the act. He simply flipped off the light switch and retreated down the hallway. April and I returned to our room and sat on our respective beds in silence, staring at the now empty tanks that had housed our pets.

April and I rode the same bus home from school. She sat with her friends, and I with mine. But on this day, she was absent, and I sat alone. Whether it was spring or fall or winter, I cannot recall. As the bus approached the neighborhood, the black iron gates opened. They provided little protection and only a ruse of escape. The gatehouse attendant waved the driver through as he began his task of returning the many children to their homes. The large and beautiful houses passed by outside the window. I imagined what the inside of each one looked like and wondered if they were similar to mine.

The bus trudged down the hills and around the lakes. I breathed my breath onto the frosted window and pressed my forehead against the cool glass. As a child, I shouldn't have known to ponder the woes of a family, but I recall giving much thought to the day-to-day life of the children on that bus. I watched each one depart down the black rubber stairs and rush to their front door or into the arms of their mom or dad. I wondered what happened when the door closed behind them. Did they hold their breath while tiptoeing past their father, or did they watch as their brother ensured he hadn't made a mistake with his chores, knowing that the consequences would propel another night of chaos? Better yet, were their hamsters living out their days happily running on the wheels inside their cages?

Utter dread seized me as the bus stopped at the top of my street. It was my turn to make my way alone, to the brick house at the end of the cul-de-sac. As I lifted my head from the window, I knew the answer.

My house was unlike those of my classmates, although no different from the houses before: filled with chaos. The outward facades deceptively hid the terror and pain inside all the pretty houses.

40

Built from Straw

After just two years in Indiana, we settled into an unremarkable house in North Carolina. Perhaps the warmth of the southern wind would break through our spirits and the gloom we'd felt in Indiana. It's been said that a house built from brick will stand the test of time, yet one built from straw will surely fall. Soon, we would know what ours was made of.

I considered myself to be a typical child. I rode bikes and made friends with the kids nearby. Meanwhile, the tomboy that was inherently inside me continued to blossom. My mom often said that I didn't get dirty, but that dirt found me. Little wonder, as I spent much of my time at the creek across the street. My playmates and I would splash in the cool water and climb the high pines that left sap clinging to my hands and hair.

As I search my memory of the unremarkable house, only one room stands out: the dining room. Dan promised not to run away again after my parents spent days searching for him in Indiana. They finally found him living in a wooden hunting blind in the forest, not far from our house. Now he'd taken up a new hobby: collecting snakes. In the backyard, among the trees and poison sumac, he'd captured a black racer. My mom humored him and purchased a heat rock to help him create the perfect terrarium. Dan liked to take the snake out when my parents were at work and place it on the dining room table. I was fascinated as I ran my fingers along its scaly body. Its sparkly eyes watched me as it slithered along the dark stained oak.

Later, in that same dining room, I remember my dad kneeling in front of me as he explained that he couldn't remember where our new apartment was and sweetly asked me to recite the address. I

obediently and unwittingly divulged the

information as I glanced over his shoulder and

looked at the table where the black snake had

hissed at me just days earlier.

The townhouse was just outside the city and nestled

between rows of identical houses in a new

subdivision. The complex's clubhouse was full of

events that even a young girl was able to attend.

Much to my delight, there was a pool as well.

Swimming was the only other thing I loved as much

as singing. I'd rush home from school every day and

put on my "baby suit," still too little to pronounce

bathing suit correctly, and beg April to take me to the

pool.

To my mother's dismay, the townhouse that was a

perfect place for a single parent with four kids

became overcrowded when my dad forced her to

allow him to live there as well. My mother hadn't

punished me for revealing her plans. I was a good

daughter who didn't lie to her parents. I learned

early on that lying was forbidden. The remedy to

any lie that fell from our lips was rewarded with a

mouthful of soap.

I recall one day while playing with my sister, when

she and I were still little enough to play, we teased

and argued as siblings do, but April ran off to tattle.

When my mom confronted me, I fibbed. She grabbed

my arm and pulled me into the kitchen. Standing at

the sink, she retrieved the bottle of liquid soap and

poured it generously into my mouth. I cried and

choked on the burn of the liquid and coughed up

bubbles that floated into the air. My mother

chuckled at my dramatics and retrieved a cup of

milk to wash out the taste. I looked down at the

bubbles in the fresh cold beverage and gagged at the mixture of Palmolive and the sour of the milk.

Another time when April and I had argued, my father snatched me up by the arm and led me into the bathroom. Tears and apologies were not going to save me from this. He pulled down my pants so that the heat from his swat would be sure to make contact with the bare skin of my cheek. He swiftly leaned me over his lap and began wildly spanking. Through my tears, I looked up to see his red face smiling with each smack. There would be no use of the 2x4s on me, where I'd be required to bend over and grab my ankles to brace myself, as I'd seen my brothers endure too many times. I wouldn't have to quiver at hearing the snap of my dad's belt or remember which shoes he'd worn that day and hope they weren't the boots with the metal tips. I was safe from the cruelty he doled out on Bryan and Dan.

My time living in the townhouse was nothing short of madness. The cops regularly came to investigate disturbances that our neighbors undoubtedly heard through the walls. My father's calm demeanor gave no hint at the dented wall behind him, a reminder to my mother's head that she should not make pot roast when he requested meatloaf. I was far too young to stand up for anyone or to put a stop to the abuse. My place was that of a mere observer, where I could do nothing to prevent the demise of my family. Upon entering the front door, my dad created a tension that was thick enough to make one feel as though they were walking through a pond of quicksand. We were indeed sinking.

One ordinary day, my mom arrived at my school. I was excited to get picked up in the middle of the day! We must be going on another adventure, I thought. It must be a surprise, but it wasn't anyone's birthday that I could think of, and my mom never

sprung us out of school early. She held my hand as

we walked the path from the brick building to the

curb, where a red hatchback waited for us. In the

driver's seat was a young woman with long

strawberry blond hair. She smiled as my mom

introduced her.

"This is Linda, my friend from work," my mom

explained.

We said our hellos as I climbed in the back. Linda

placed the car into gear, and we sped off, making our

way to her apartment.

My mom and I sat on the couch as Linda pretended

to tidy up, making believe we were having a private

moment.

"I need you to be my brave little girl," my mom said

as she held both my hands. "Your brothers are home

now, packing up our things. I'm leaving your dad,"

she said with resolve.

I could see that she was asking herself to be brave

too. I smiled as I agreed to her request. Just then the

phone rang. Linda brought the receiver to her ear

but quickly slammed it down.

"We've got to go! He knows you're here," she said in a

hurried tone.

We frantically jumped into the red hatchback. I

could feel the gears shifting as we turned abruptly

onto side streets and down alleyways, making sure

that we weren't being followed. We made a quick

switch, and I was off again, this time with my mom's

friend Dina. She immediately made me feel safe. Her

big green eyes matched her wide smile that seemed

to fill the car with warmth and comfort.

The next stop was April's school. It felt like a whirlwind of excitement and apprehension. The minutes passed like seconds, and my head spun as I tried to make sense of the mixture of emotions I felt. We were finally going to be free, and yet sadness and fear swarmed inside me. There was no time to brace for impact. A rush of adrenaline propelled me forward and hid me away from the tears that were certain to come.

The only information my sister received was to wait outside for someone named Dina. In the eighties, schools were much less secure. All that was required was a simple phone call that a friend of your parents was picking you up and that was good enough for the school receptionist.

My mother taught us not to ever go anywhere with a stranger, so when we pulled up to see April innocently standing there, she asked Dina for the secret password that only my family knew. Dina was by all definitions a stranger to us. Although April locked eyes with me, the password was still required. Dina stammered, cussing a bit and slammed her hand on the steering wheel. Finally she pushed the word that sounded like gibberish off her lips. "Stada Baba!" And with that, April climbed in the car.

Now the three of us made our way over to pick up my brothers. The car slowed as we neared the entrance to the townhouse development. Bryan and Dan stood waiting with several large black garbage bags. Their faces were solemn. Dan's hinted a tint of red that gave way to the notion that he'd been crying. In contrast, Bryan muted any expression that would have deemed him anything less than brave and in charge. The boys loaded up the trunk, and we were on our way again.

Dina tried to play down the drama as she asked us all about school. No amount of small talk was going to cut the tension or redirect the vast array of emotions we held inside us. Much like a carbonated beverage that's been shaken so that the fizz from the liquid bubbled just under the surface, our emotions churned and simmered. As evening was nearing, we pulled into the drive of an unfamiliar house in a quaint neighborhood. We each retrieved a garbage bag from the trunk and heaved them inside, where my mom stood waiting for us. We embraced all at once, enveloping one another in a group hug as our hearts pounded with fear and

relief.

The four of us kids gathered around the coffee table in the stranger's house who'd given us refuge. By nightfall our tension started to ease. Typically, for children, the only logical thing to follow was hunger!

A long-awaited pizza delivery driver dropped off two large pies. It was eerily quiet, but as we bit into the cheesy pie and crisp pepperoni, Dan threw the first joke. It was something unremarkable and unmemorable, but the awkwardness faded as we all broke into laughter.

We sat in the glow of the TV light with the empty boxes that contained only an abandoned pie crust or two. It was a welcome quiet, with only the hum of chatter among the adults. Every now and again, I'd catch my mom glancing over her shoulder at us with a weary smile. It felt as though it could have been almost any other day. However, the pizza would prove to be one of the last meals that the four of us would ever eat together again.

Suddenly there was a knock at the door. The hosts of the house looked knowingly at my mother. Then a recognizable voice calmly said, "Pam?"

The knocking grew louder as the voice grew colder.

He repeated, "Pam, open the door, Pam. I just want to talk to you."

Louder knocking and then kicking. "Pam, open the door. OPEN THE DOOR, PAM!"

April and I ran upstairs and locked ourselves in the bathroom. Meanwhile, Dan was hiding in the room next door. We could hear the banging and kicking and knocking and then, silence. Had he gone? Maybe he'd given up. We peered out the window below and in the grass, under the bright moonlight, we spotted my dad. He was crawling on his hands and knees with what appeared to be a shiny object in his mouth. A knife!

Just then I heard Dan. At thirteen, he sobbed. A guttural and wrenching cry that made me shutter. A cry that housed such pain, that it could easily have been your own and you would not have known the difference. My ambivalence of love and fear for my

father had muted my own tears. So I cried for Dan,

who would never be the same.

We returned to our townhouse the next day to

collect the rest of what we could manage to put into

more black garbage bags, only to find that my dad

had beaten us there. He'd sliced open his and my

mom's waterbed, leading to a flood down the stairs

amongst the broken objects. Nothing was off limits.

Toys and books were destroyed and scattered

throughout the house. A tidal wave of rage had

ripped through our home and left nothing but

disaster.

My mom swiftly secured a new home across town,

where my dad wouldn't be able to find us and with

the hope we could finally have the chance to be

children. Dina had united us in the brick split level.

It was like inheriting a new sister. She occupied the

open space downstairs that contained a family room, complete with a private bedroom and full bath.

A small black-and-white TV sat on her bedside table and in the other corner was a large stereo. Concert tickets were stuffed into oversized glass jars, and I imagined what it was like to live so freely. Dina often joined in as we cranked up a new band called Bon Jovi and danced around while pretending to be rock star backup singers. Many nights while my mother worked late, Dina would dial up the local pizza place and order our go-to pepperoni pizza.

One Saturday afternoon as I played with Mickey, I grabbed a hot dog and took a bite. Mickey knew a variety of tricks, but my favorite was when he sat on his hind legs and begged. I peeled off a piece of the hot dog and demanded he beg. He obliged and gobbled up the piece of meat. Again and again I requested a trick, and when I refused to reward him

with the last piece, he lunged at me and took hold of

my left cheek. The next thing I knew, April had flung

him off me and he landed on the floor with a thud.

Dina came rushing up the stairs to investigate the

commotion. Blood began flowing down my face.

Dina led me to the bathroom and pressed a cold

washcloth over the wound. By the time my mother

returned home from work, my face had swollen up

by two sizes and I could only see out of my right eye.

The next morning I lay on the metal exam table as

the doctor explained that I would need laser surgery

to close the gaping hole in my cheek. The bite

narrowly missed my eye; yet as the needle came

down to numb my cheek, I panicked. Several nurses

rushed in to hold me down, and I squeezed my eyes

shut so the needle wouldn't accidentally blind me.

Mickey changed after that. He would growl if anyone

walked near him while he was eating. I quit playing with our beloved family pet who had brought me such joy just a few years earlier. It seemed everyone was spinning inside their own orbit, leaving little time for a dog.

I found myself looking for solace, and walks became my outlet. Walks in the woods, walks on the way home from school, walks when I was lonely. Then one afternoon as I explored the neighborhood, I spotted a beautiful red sports car. In those days, strange cars that didn't belong in your neighborhood weren't quite the red flag that they are today. A seven-year-old could walk alone without much worry of being kidnapped, so it didn't occur to me that there was any danger looming. The car slowed and soon it was driving alongside me. Then I heard a voice I recognized call out. "Hey, kiddo."

"Um, hi. What are you doing here?" I asked with caution.

"Oh, I was just test-driving this car. Do you live around here?" my dad asked slyly.

"Uh, I-I was just going for a walk, but I need to g-go home now," I stammered.

"Well, I can give you a ride. Why don't you hop in, and I'll take you home? Which house is yours?" he inquired.

My mom made it clear that we were not to ever tell anyone about my dad. We were never to speak of personal matters that occurred inside the house or within the family. Most importantly, if we saw my dad, we were not to say where we lived. She was very careful to make sure that I knew the rules, especially after the dining room disaster, where I innocently divulged my mom's secret plan and my dad cunningly tricked me into telling him of the location of the new house.

"I don't live around here. I was visiting a friend," I told him confidently.

Then, as though my feet had a mind of their own, they found the next right-hand turn, down a street that wasn't mine, to a house I didn't live in. I stood on the stoop as he drove down the street and made a U-turn, passing me once again.

It was hard running home with my throat closing up and my stomach in my chest and legs that felt like a card deck that was moments away from crumbling. I ran through the woods where no red sports cars could go and came in through the back door where Bryan was standing in the kitchen. He'd recently turned eighteen and found a little place of his own, so I was happily surprised to see him. I heaved my shaking arms around him, relieved that our

protector had returned.

Just then my mom appeared in the doorway. My

words rushed out as I relayed the unnerving

encounter with my father. She seemed unsurprised

that he tracked us down, and unbeknownst to me at

the time, he'd been calling her endlessly and

harassing her at work. She nonchalantly stated that

the shiny red sports car likely wasn't his and that I'd

done the right thing. I kept a watchful eye out for

weeks afterward. The long walks I enjoyed and the

security I had begun to feel was replaced with a

familiar worry. Rarely did I leave the yard after the

incident. Besides, Bryan seemed to be spending

more and more time at our house, and I didn't mind

having him there to look after us.

As it turned out, he was secretly tending to Dan. The

drug-induced escape was much more dangerous

than the wooden hideout he escaped to in the past

or his collection of hissing snakes. One evening the

police appeared at the door and took Dan away. I

couldn't understand where he went or why he

hadn't come home when we moved again soon

afterward.

The Trailer

62

It's a fallacy that tornadoes are attracted to trailer parks. Trailers aren't built to weather its enormity or stand a blast of that magnitude. The tornado knows not a trailer from a mansion, a wood cabin from a ranch, a cottage from a Tudor, but when it comes through and smashes your life to bits, no matter the house, your home is still destroyed.

It wasn't until several months had passed and two moves later that I would see Dan again, in a small two-bedroom trailer with a wooden porch attached to its side. The trailer where we gave away Mickey to a sweet old couple, and Dina moved into her own apartment, leaving just the "girls" to occupy its cramped space.

Despite ongoing health ailments, my mom added on two more jobs. I'd watch her in the mornings carefully applying mascara and pink lipstick with her shaky hands as her blond hair bounced out of the hot rollers. With a finishing spray of Aqua Net, she'd be off to work again.

There wasn't much to look forward to in those days. I'd make my way through the trailer park to the bus stop with my holey shoes, wet from the morning dew. My feet would ache as I squished them under the heat of the bus, which did little to dry them prior to stepping through the door of my classroom. April and I would return home at the end of the day with hunger pangs and scour the cabinets for an afterschool snack. With limited selection, we created our own out of marshmallow fluff. We'd grab one bowl and blob the marshmallow in. Then for thirty seconds we'd watch the fluff growing through the yellow light and listen to the hum of the

waves working their magic. When the timer

exhausted itself and three beeps rang out, a hard

marshmallow mound was ready to be devoured. It

was pure sugar, but something to put in our empty

bellies before round two of the kitchen search.

For dinner, we were faced with the challenge of

deciding which was better, Suddenly Salad or peanut

butter and grape jelly sandwiches. There weren't

many choices at the food bank. A staple of

selections, and if you were lucky, you would get the

boxed salad; a cold pasta dish that was ready in

minutes. A dish that two young girls could make on

their own. Far too many meals consisted of greasy

peanut butter on stale white bread with bitter

chunks of imposter grapes. I remember the goo

dripping out of the folds of the bread and lapping up

every last bit in an effort to fill myself before I lay

down with the restlessness of hunger. To this day, I have not eaten a peanut butter and jelly sandwich. Some memories are not nostalgic. They taste like the bitter loneliness of a once full family that now has become the taste of starvation.

The trailer was the last time I saw my father. Bryan accompanied my mom, my sister, and me over to wherever my dad had ended up living for the moment. My mom was desperate for money, and without any child support, there wasn't much hope. This time, my father had promised her that he had money for his children, who deserved a reprieve from dinners of food bank leftovers.

When we arrived, he appeared ragged, and even as a young girl, I knew the smell of alcohol that wisped out at the end of each of his words. My mom tried her best to exchange pleasantries, but because she was a bold and blunt woman, she got right to the point of our visit. *Money, where was the money?* Her

children were hungry, and she had bills to pay. He

reached in his pockets, but empty hands returned.

He laughed the laugh of a person who was no longer

part of reality, our reality.

Despite the warm temperature and the humidity

clinging to the night air, April and I rolled up the

back windows. It was as if there were a sudden chill

that brought with it a whispered warning. Just then,

he crossed his arms and leaned into my mother's

window. Suddenly, Bryan jumped out of the

passenger door and ran toward my father. My dad

stood upright with surprise.

I remember the whole thing in slow motion. Bryan's

long right hook flew up to meet my father's five-nine

frame, delivering an overdue punch to the face. The

contact of fist to cheek. Strands of red from his

poorly combed-over hair stood on its roots, the toes

of his boots rose off the dusty ground, and then my dad landed with a thud.

Bryan stood over him as my mom yelled from the window.

"Larry, Larry, are you okay? Larry, are you dead? Bryan, shake him and see if he's all right."

And then . . . a snore. Bryan had knocked him out cold! My father's reward for leaning in the car and groping my mother out of sight of her two daughters.

My mom hadn't shown any fear at the confrontation or at seeing her ex-husband, her stalker and abuser. I can only imagine how she gathered the courage to ask this man for money, which is why I still remember that she started laughing! She laughed so loud and so hard, she doubled over the steering wheel, gasping through tears of joy! She laughed a satisfied laugh. Bryan returned to the car, and we sped away before my father could wake from his stupor. Later, he told Bryan that he was so inebriated, he didn't remember the meeting at all.

We abandoned all hope that my father would provide any assistance and continued on as we'd done the many days and nights before. I'd brush my teeth and put on my pajamas and soon I'd be asleep, long before my mom would appear again. I took to writing her notes every night. This became my remedy for the longing I had to be with her. I'd secretly fold the note and place it inside her pillowcase. I imagined her head resting on my letter and hearing the crinkle of the page as she adjusted her weary body and prepared for another long day ahead. In the mornings she'd say that she got my note and that she missed me too.

Then one day, Dan came home. He was not the funny Dan I remembered, but an angry teen filled with venom. At every turn he tested my mother and picked arguments with my sister. I grew afraid of him and wrote a note to my mom one night that Dan had slapped April. He must have been watching me through the crack of my mom's bedroom door because he barged in, tearing at my hands and knocking over the lamp that sat on the bedside table, an innocent victim to the drama that ensued.

He was wrestling with me as I did my best to fight him away. Just as he was about to strike me, April ran in, yelling for him to leave. The argument continued to the living room, but not before I quickly shoved the note under the blanket and tucked it neatly into the bed frame. The next morning, Dan was gone.

There were no birthday gifts that year. My mother, unable to afford time off from work, handed the duty off to Dina, who seemed only too pleased to entertain me for my special day. I donned my favorite red velvet dress that I had easily outgrown a year or two prior. Dina honored my request for dinner at Red Lobster. I'd seen the commercials. In my young mind, it looked as if it was the fanciest place one could hope to spend their birthday! The restaurant bustled with patrons as the waitstaff endlessly danced down the isles with trays of steaming lobster and shrimp with melted butter. It was lively, and because it happened to be Valentine's Day, it was crowded with couples and noise reminiscent of a loud family of six. A chocolate cake was placed in front of me with a single flaming candle. My wish was that I alone could fix the broken pieces of our hearts that would make us a family once more.

On my wall hangs a photograph of the four of us kids at the trailer on the wooden porch, smiling and hugging. Me always the ham, with a bubble of pink gum balancing on my lips. It portrays a happy family that we truly had never been, but it captured a moment where we could have been those people. A moment where we all pretended to be.

The Many Small Apartments

It became the norm to move from one side of town, then back, and then back again. Schools would no longer tell me goodbye, but see you later, since I would always return midyear. I lost track of the number of moves in the five years in North Carolina. Was it six or seven, or eight, maybe nine? I couldn't be sure because it always ended the same. We'd flee in hopes of escaping my father's relentless stalking, only to have him threaten my mom in some manner before we packed up once more.

While living in the trailer, he dropped off a half dozen roses with razor blades inside each flower for my mother. He continued to call her jobs and yell at her bosses, sometimes leading to her termination.

He'd given her number to various jail cellmates, who would call her at work and sometimes our house and would say something inappropriate to one of the young girls who answered the phone. For much of the time after that, I was no longer allowed to answer a ring, which sometimes was incessant for hours.

The last of the many small apartments brought back both of my brothers for a time, but never at the same time. Meanwhile, April had become a teenager. Unfortunately for her, her little sister had not. I was always happy to go anywhere with my siblings, even

if it was to a party none of us should have been at.

I followed April and Bryan up the stairs and entered

a room full of party participants. One man was on

the floor, and he clearly had been partaking in

something I didn't quite understand. He was

mumbling and grabbed my leg as I passed. I wasn't

sure what to do, but I managed to yank my calf free

from his drug-induced grip. I found April and Bryan

talking with a group of friends. My nerves were

calling out for me to leave, but I was trapped. I

headed for the bathroom in order to contain myself,

only to find a tray of white powder on the counter.

Thanks to endless after school specials, I recognized

it as cocaine. Moments later I passed back by April

and Bryan and headed for the van to escape. As I

pulled back the door, I spotted Dan and my sister's

friend with a bag of pills. They both offered me

something called speed, but in the era of "Just Say No," I did.

The next day I told my mom what April had been up to while she was at work, only to receive a spanking with the wooden spoon. The swatting left bruises wherever it landed, which was everywhere. It was the newest addition to my mom's punishments after realizing she could no longer force me to drink the Palmolive. The lesson was easily learned. My mother didn't want to know that another one of her children had started to falter. Her divorce was just finalized, and she embraced her newfound freedom, sowing her wild oats, she'd say. She resigned herself to saving no one. She'd just barely saved herself.

That was the only time I ratted out my sister. She too made me pay, by ostracizing me from her inner world, despite the fact that she was still responsible for my well-being. As teenagers do, she rebelled. She fled her status as a straight A student for something

a little more interesting: boys! She was faced with

few choices, including abandoning me altogether or

taking me along despite her resentment. It was

apparent that I was no longer going to impede her

independence and freedom. I went from being her

favorite playmate to a menace and obligation. Bryan

too had become weary of his role as the protector,

and he and April grew close, leaving me to fend for

myself.

I knew that I'd betrayed April and felt that I lost her.

She was my one constant in a life where I was never

sure who would be there tomorrow or what would

happen. The siblings we once had been to one

another seemed unattainable now. The isolation

drug on, as did the parties. There was no way for me

to escape the past, and there was no escaping the

present. In wanting to be a part of April's inner

circle again, I accepted the tid-bits of inclusion, even if it did mean saying yes to alcohol. Who cared if I got drunk anyway.

Just three years ago I had a family, or at least my siblings, but now I was alone. Despite having a few friends, I'd often ride my bike to the creek and sit for hours and contemplate what could have been. If only they knew how much I loved them, they would surely come back and return to the people I yearned for them to be again. The trickle along the winding bank didn't reveal any answers. If only I could tell my friends and confide in them, maybe I wouldn't feel so alone, I thought. If only I could talk to someone. I knew the rules, and I knew that my mother wouldn't be pleased if I "opened a can of worms." So, when the streetlights blinked on, I'd return home and try to understand the feeling that I had no words to describe.

I was too young and incapable of saving anyone. My prayers had gone unanswered and birthday wishes had yet to come true. Although I feared the days when my father terrorized us endlessly, leading to beatings of whoever was in reach, my heart still longed for the closeness of a full house. Like a cold rain on the brink of sleet, the loneliness showered over me and peppered me with sadness. I longed for my sister, who was once the other pea in my pod. I missed the boy with the many talents who loved to make his siblings laugh with his impersonations and the brother who protected us. Blind ears and eyes surrounded me, and I resolved that there was only one solution to end the nagging ache inside my heart.

On top of the dusty refrigerator sat a long shotgun, and because I was home by myself yet again, I stood in the kitchen eyeing it. Minutes passed as I stared at the long barrel. I climbed on top of the brown counter above the cabinets and reached my small arm toward the gun. Slowly lowering it down, I climbed onto the kitchen floor and sat with the gun across my lap. I did not give thought as to who might miss me or of the mess it might make in my mother's clean home.

I thought of the pain of abandonment and the heartache I imagined no one could know. I thought of April and how she no longer saw me as the sister she loved to play with, but as a nuisance who hindered her from the parties and boys she had happily traded me for. I thought of Dan, who no longer laughed, his face hidden behind the spray paint he huffed and the encounter where he touched me where he shouldn't have. I thought of Bryan, now the other pea to April's pod. I thought of my mom, who I missed so many nights. She had replaced her three jobs for one, only to spend her free time with her boyfriend, who didn't want a little girl tagging along. And I thought of the man who I once called Dad. The man who prevented my happiness and who tore our family apart, as though we lived inside a straw house that crumbled in the wind. Why wasn't my love enough to save them? Why didn't they love me enough to save themselves?

Then with the cold barrel of the gun to my left temple, my small arms already weak from its weight, I searched for the trigger. I fumbled with my right hand and then placed my finger on the steel arc that would end the feeling I couldn't quite name. I closed my eyes and pulled. For a moment I waited, expecting a loud burst and the resolution to my pain, but the quiet of the empty kitchen remained. Lowering the barrel from my head, I calmly returned it to its resting place atop the refrigerator, where no one would know that it had been removed.

The feeling tormented me and the following summer I would try to escape it again.

It wasn't long after the day with the shotgun when David moved in. He'd recently lost his house in a fire and was a welcome addition in our small apartment. He was the first person my mom dated who truly seemed to want me around. Their first date consisted of taking us to the state fair where he filled our hands with crisp twenties and sent us off to enjoy the rides and fair food. Albeit a good way for some adult alone time, but despite that, I liked David. He was thirteen years younger than my mother and was not only funny, but calm. That was something unfamiliar to me, but a welcome reprieve to the chaos I'd grown accustomed to.

The night of the fire, he had promised to take me roller skating. He made it up later down the road and even though I don't remember the event, what stands out is that he didn't let me down. David also brought my mom home. With his financial help and their relationship, the parties subsided and I was once again free again to be a child. However now, with too much knowledge of the world's sins and its temptations, I found it impossible to return to the girl I had been.

At the end of my fifth grade year, the school put on a dance for the graduating class. A cute boy asked to accompany me, and I was beyond excited for my first real dance. April tended to my hair and even allowed me to borrow one of her skirts. I matched it with a crisp white shirt that was lined with pretty lace around the collar and sleeves. Once I was dressed, I excitedly tromped downstairs. The dance started early, so I quickly made a sandwich. I stepped outside into the warmth of the late May afternoon and bit into the soft bread. My mouth filled with

spicy mustard and the sweetness of the ham.

Just then a car approached, and Dan stepped out.

He'd been staying with us off and on, but was never

really home. Our two bedrooms didn't leave much

space, and the couch was not convenient for a

nightly slumber. As he walked toward me, I

swallowed a bite of the sandwich, ready to show off

my perfect outfit for my perfect "adult" dance.

"Where did you get that?" he asked.

"Wha?" I mumbled with a full mouth. "The

sandwich? I made it."

His voice grew angry. "Did you get that from the

bottom shelf? That's mine!"

Before I could answer, he slapped me across my face

and my sandwich flew from my hand, but not before

It doused my pristine white shirt, staining it with

streaks of mustard. Tears burned my eyes, which

paired well with the sting on my cheek.

April ran out, already knowing what the commotion

was, at the sight of Dan. She breezed past him with

an evil look as she dashed over to me. She saw my

tears, the mustard, and my quivering lip and took

me by the hand and led me inside. We found Dan

standing in the kitchen, smirking and eating a ham

sandwich. No apologies were given and no other

words were said.

Upstairs we found an alternative to the shirt and

paired it with a different skirt that April picked out

from her side of the closet. When I returned

downstairs, my mother greeted me. Dan had already

filled her in on the sandwich incident and the

wardrobe change. That was the last time I ever saw

him. For the next ten years I couldn't stand the taste

of mustard. I was always reminded of that moment

and relived the snowball of emotions ranging from blaming myself to fear and the sadness I felt at losing my brother.

The last day of school came to a close, and once more we packed our belongings and headed north for a fresh start. My mom, David, April, and me. A new family to a new state, destination unknown. That summer we stayed with Grandma in her small trailer in Indiana. It wasn't adequate enough for a pair of adults and two butting sisters, so David set up a tent outside in the yard and tried his best to convince us that it was just like camping. The new family unit did little to curb the feeling I couldn't name. With two siblings left behind in North Carolina, I spent most of my time pining for the people I no longer knew and learning to live with the unresolved.

Before summer wound to a close, a package arrived on my grandma's front porch. A package addressed to me. It was wrapped in crisp brown paper with no return address, just the notation "From: Dad." My mom looked at it in horror and I, too afraid to open the contents, placed it on the old brown carpet of the living room floor. David retrieved it and bravely took it outside. We waited—for what, we didn't know. He returned with a colorful box that contained Princess Barbie. I stared at the gift that I did not ask for and had not wanted. I was conflicted with emotions and almost insulted that my dad would buy a Barbie for his tomboy daughter. However, the audacity was underwhelmed by the fear that he knew where to deliver it.

The Yellow Duplex

The yellow duplex sat on a rolling hill on the edge of town. With only two bedrooms, it was just enough room for the four of us. By far the best feature was the laundry chute! I was shamelessly amused by it. In its newness, I'd shove clean clothes and stuffed animals in the chute and race down one flight of stairs. Then I'd fly across the blue carpet that spanned throughout the living room and over the dull brown tiles in the small galley kitchen. When I reached the wooden sliding door that separated the kitchen from the stairs to the basement, I'd fling it open, smashing it back into the wall. Finally I'd take the stairs two by two, only to find lumps of clothes and toys patiently waiting for me to retrieve them.

We easily settled into family life with David. He worked a nine to five as a mechanic, while my mom worked the phones from home doing sales. It had been a long time since I had the privilege of returning from school and seeing my mom there waiting for me. As I started my first experience with Junior High, I wasn't prepared for the giggles or the scrutiny my southern accent would bring.

Middle school isn't easy for most, and I had unfortunately encountered my awkward phase. My blond locks morphed into a mousy brown that hinged on the verge of gray. I had a slender form with an over-sized behind, and in those days that was something to be made fun of and not be admired for. Eventually I made a couple of friends and found ways to enjoy my new surroundings, including being able to walk to Lake Michigan.

I spent much of my free time along the shoreline. At the pier, my friends and I played a game of wet or dry. The goal was to make it from the base of the pier to the end that stretched out toward the lake, without getting wet. I'd stand at the shore and watch for my chance as I watched the waves splash up and over the pier, drenching the cement every several feet. When I saw the lake begin to recede, I bolted toward the pier, abruptly stopping before a wave jumped up in front of my face and smacked down on the other side. I ran as fast as I could go before I heard the force of another wave blast down behind me. My heart raced, knowing that it just nearly missed me. Unharmed I reached the end where my friends were waiting. We celebrated by running back down again. Had I been a wiser child, I would have known that this was less of a game of wet or dry and more a test of fate. But when you're young, you're blessed as well as cursed with perceived invincibility.

When the weather became warm enough, I'd often take a detour on my way home from school. I'd climb down the loose sand on the face of the bluff where I could access the waterfront for a quick dip. The lake appeared endless and spread out in every direction. The water called to me like an old friend. Sometimes I jumped in jeans and all! I loved surfing the waves as they lifted me up and hauled me to shore. The water was my happy place, but what came next was something I never knew I wanted.

At forty-one, my mother found herself pregnant. April and I were excited, and we quickly determined that it was to be a boy. The four of us agreed that he would be called Zach and it was settled immediately. Not long after, our intuition proved to be correct, and we began to plan for our new baby brother.

My mom's pregnancy was risky due to her age, and she found herself in the hospital more than at home.

I'd often make the trek up the many hills of the

small town to the hospital room where the staff

came to know me by first name. First, I'd check in to

see if she was awake, and upon finding her sleeping,

I'd pad down the hallway to the OB waiting room. It

was filled with a variety of snacks for visitors.

Although it was the middle of summer, the packet of

"cup o' noodle" soup, called to me. Once I located the

remote and turned on the TV, it was time to settle in

and wait for the familiar alarms that notified the

nurses of an emergency. I'd peek out from the

doorway to see a sea of scrubs running to my

mother's room and minutes later they would calmly

evacuate, which would prompt me to know that she

was stabilized.

Once I knew she was awake, I'd sit by her bedside

and tell her about the weather and what chores I'd

completed. She'd ask about my friends and if there

were any cute boys I liked at school. I treasured

those hours with my mom, just her and me. Before I

knew it, David would come in with his blue work

shirt that read "Dave" on the tattered pocket. I'd kiss

my mom's cheek and tell Zach to be good and to

"cook" longer, before I made my way back to the

yellow duplex.

Just like the days before, I did the familiar routine:

chores, walk, soup, TV, wait. Then the alarm rang

out, but this time the nurses didn't calmly exit my

mom's room. I peered around the corner to see

them wheeling her down the hallway. Her doctor

approached me and asked that I call David

immediately. They were taking her to surgery. The

baby could wait no longer. I dialed the house, but it

rang incessantly. I called over and over. It was a

sunny Saturday in July, and David was likely out

taking a drive, having a moment away from the

hospital and work and the responsibilities to children who weren't his.

Just as I'd almost given up and thought it better to run the mile and a half home, he appeared at the end of the hallway with April, holding a bouquet of brightly colored flowers. I told him what happened, and he raced down the hallway and disappeared for some time. April and I sat quietly in the waiting room. This wasn't good. This was too soon, almost two months too soon! What would happen to my mom? Was she okay? Would Zach make it? My hopes and fears tangled in my mind. Soon, a nurse appeared in the doorway with news. Our baby brother was in the NICU.

April and I ventured over to the glass wall where we could view the babies. Inside a clear vessel, wrapped tightly in a hospital blanket, was our new brother. The nurse appeared on the other side of the window and wheeled the transparent cradle over

for us to have a better view. At seven weeks early, his

lungs weren't quite developed, but yet he weighed

seven pounds four ounces! His skin was translucent,

and we were told that he wouldn't be ready to go

home anytime soon. I remember marveling at him,

every finger, every minute twitch and expression. At

twelve years old, I was finally a big sister!

Hours later, David accompanied my mother down

the hallway. There were complications with the

Csection and they'd almost lost her. She pulled

through and a week later, Zach made miraculous

growth! Even his lungs were completely developed

and they were both ready to go home. I reveled in

my new role as a big sister. I'd even sneak into the

room Zach shared with my mom and David, so that I

could watch him sleep. I changed diapers and

dressed him and held him when he napped. I took

him for walks in the stroller where I showed him off to my friends. "Look at how cute he is!" I'd boast. I not only adored him, but Zach was my first true love. I vowed to be there for him and to show him the unconditional love that I longed for with my siblings.

As the months passed and Zach grew out of his bassinet, he was moved to my bedroom. April and I were shuffled to the basement where David constructed a wood panel wall to separate us and give the illusion of privacy. With the small basement windows and the draft of cold winter nights, we grew restless. She would blast her radio, and I would blast mine, never agreeing on what the best genre of music was. My parents endured the mix of hip-hop and leftover hair bands. April became more distant, and although I was finally becoming a teen as well, we shared little more than the wall between us.

As a young teen still adapting to the new family, I found my own way of acting out and letting my displeasure be known. Puberty was inching its way into my moods, and I often found myself miffed by something neither my mother nor David understood. I'd take my unwanted emotions out on the sliding door that led to my basement room. The force would send the door crashing into its home in the hollow of the wall. At times I would push it so haphazardly that it would rebel too, flying back out of the wall and smashing into me.

Finally, David had had enough and duct-taped it inside its wall, leaving me to find new ways to put sound to my emotions. Because my mother would often ground me to the house where I was to wash the nightly dinner dishes, I repaid her by breaking most of her glasses and claiming it was an accident due to my clumsy hands, neither of which were true.

Before Zach's first birthday, Bryan decided to join us in Wisconsin. He would come by for short visits, but to my dismay he returned to the pod he'd formed with April. Sometimes in the middle of the night, he'd show up drunk and crying. I'd creep upstairs and see him hunched over the kitchen table as my mother sat beside him. By the time I woke for school, he'd be gone. Wisconsin would later prove to be the place he never meant to be and the place he would never escape from.

The two years spent in the yellow duplex were bittersweet. I adjusted my southern drawl to meet the Dutch-sounding northern accent and tried my best to fit in. By the end of seventh grade, I had even accumulated a close friend. I still spent time on my prized BMX bike that I received for Christmas a couple years before. I'd ride through town and find trees to climb, almost as often as I would find trouble. After learning to shoplift from an older friend in North Carolina, it wasn't unusual for me to swing by the local grocery store and find an item or two to shove down the front of my jeans. I put a stop to it after the store busted me and I endured a spanking and a well-deserved, month-long grounding. Besides, I found new hobbies in Wisconsin.

Although I joined the choir at the new school, I was thrilled to find that it also housed an Olympic-size indoor pool! Up until now I never enjoyed gym class unless we were playing Dodge ball. I was highly competitive and enjoyed showing off my agility skills, but now I couldn't wait for third period! I never missed an opportunity to swim. While most of my classmates groaned, I impatiently waited through my first and second classes until I could change into my suit and stand on the high dive. The water, paired with my passion for singing, brought me peace, even if it only lasted the length of a song.

My first experience with diving was when I was six. April was chatting with her friends while I worked on my back flip from the edge of the pool. I watched as the children climbed the tall ladder and walked to the end of the bouncy plank, jumping high before leaping off into the cool blue water beneath them.

My stomach flip-flopped and tickled as I imagined it being me. I asked April if I could try it and after agreeing, she promised to watch me.

I climbed the first three stairs, then made a misstep, smacking my knee on the hot metal ladder and peeling back a bit of skin from my shin. I quickly recovered and continued my ascent. As I approached the top, my eyes peeked over the board, and I gazed out at the long stretch. My heart excitedly raced as I increased my pace. Both feet now stood at the beginning of the board. Then without hesitation, I strutted down that thing like it was a runway and gave a little hop. My coordination wasn't quite right, and the board bounced back out of sync with my foot placement, making my knees buckle a bit. I caught my balance, plugged my nose, closed my eyes and jumped! I glided through the air, but I wasn't prepared for the impact. The splash ripped my arm upward, and I scratched my face with my fingers that were holding my nose closed and nearly punched myself in slow motion. Alarmed, I quickly swished the water and kicked as hard as my little legs would allow, all the while wondering how much longer it would take to reach the top. Finally, I emerged at the surface and made my way to the exit ladder. Then I asked April if I could do it again!

Now I worked on my form and challenged myself to swim the length of the pool in one breath. The teacher praised my natural ability and there was

mention that if I chose to join the swim team, I could

have a chance to compete in the Olympics. Although

I liked the idea of competition, it was in the water,

amongst the sounds of the splashing and the whistle

from the coach, that I was able to quiet my mind. It

was where I found forgiveness for my inability to

make any headway at saving my family.

Meanwhile, two of my classmates and I had been

rehearsing for a national singing competition in

Milwaukee. We practiced for months and finally it

was time for the performance. The concert hall was

filled with other children my age, as well as older

peers from various parts of the country. I remember

standing in the acoustic room and seeing my

parents sitting in front of me in metal folding chairs.

My mother held the program in her hands and I

tried to imagine that she wasn't looking at me.

I began to sing in key of A, and I felt the familiar numbness in my fingers, accompanied by shaky knees, but I was determined to overcome my fear. I focused on my breath as I pierced the room with the note. The pitch and clarity came swirling out as I carefully listened to the three of us harmonize as we sang. The practice had paid off! I can still hear the melody in my head and recall the lyrics. "My heart's in the highland and chasing a deer. Chasing the wild deer and following the row. My heart's in the highlands, wherever I roam."

When the song finished, my parents smiled proudly and clapped as they approached us with congratulations. My mom wrapped an arm around my shoulder and gave a squeeze.

"That was amazing! I had no idea you could sing like that!!" she said.

I shrugged her away, embarrassed.

When all of the participants had finished with their pieces and arrangements, we waited for the winners to be announced. I hadn't entered the competition with the expectation of winning or even the desire to win. I'd entered it to prove to myself that I could overcome my stage fright. The winners were announced, and to my disbelief, we were awarded a bronze medal in the "best trio" category! I proudly hung the medal from the mirror of my wooden dresser and every morning as I dressed for school, I'd trace the pointed edges. The medal was a keepsake of not only my accomplishment, but a reminder of the possibilities if I chose to be brave enough to confront my fears.

Music would stay with me through the years, providing comfort and an escape in the songs I crafted. My own music therapy that stilled the depths of my sadness. I drew out lyrics on old notebooks and napkins and quietly sang them to myself as I considered what my future might be. My dreams of being a diver ended when Bryan was sentenced to prison. The shame was more than enough motivation to send us driving to the other side of the country.

The Full House and One Truck Camper

We arrived in Boise just days after the end of seventh grade. David had a job waiting for him there, but it didn't take long for my mother to decide that the one pine tree in the city wasn't enough for her to find happiness. So, we kept driving. We wound through the mountains as the hum of the truck chugged up and down the slopes of the cliffs and past little towns with no names.

I sat alongside David in the truck. My mom, April, and Zach followed in the car behind. I liked riding with David. We didn't have much to talk about, but he let me pick which song to listen to on the radio. There was no awkwardness, just a good tune coming through the speakers that I'd sing along with while he tapped his finger in rhythm on the steering wheel. He and my mother had only been married a short time, but I was happy he was a part of our lives and that I was a daughter to a man who genuinely cared for me.

I did not want to leave Wisconsin. I didn't want to move again. I was growing tired of being the new kid in school, with new friends and a new house and a new town to learn. I hadn't realized until living in Wisconsin what a luxury it was just to know what the front door to my home looked like. I didn't even like the name "Idaho" or the long drive to get there. I made this abundantly clear to my parents: by my many mood swings, rolling my eyes, and flipping my hair. I'd just come into puberty, and the abrupt change after two years of stability did not agree with my fluctuating hormones.

Finally, we arrived in a little town near a beautiful lake. The backdrop of the mountains enveloped the water's edge and I was awestruck at its beauty, in spite of myself. In a matter of hours, David got a job. With the costs involved in moving, my parents were short on funds to secure any housing and so they came up with a solution. Welcome the truck camper!

On the outskirts of town sat a little campground equipped with a trailer that provided private showers and indoor toilets, as the camper didn't house either of these necessities. The five of us lived out the remainder of the summer there. It was uncomfortably crowded, and so April and I spent as much time as we could at the lake. We again bonded, but this time over boys. I was finally old enough to talk to her about them and she finally trusted me enough to divulge her secrets. So just a few months after arriving in Idaho, while we waited for my parents to return from Wisconsin with our old items to fill our new house on the side of the mountain, she honored me with a big one. She was pregnant!

Not long after, she revealed her pregnancy to my mom and David. Then, without notice, April moved into a house for pregnant teens. It wasn't because of my parents' shame, but because of April's stubborn way of rebelling against their disappointment. I missed her terribly, and on the weekends I'd go to visit her. We'd spend the day talking about the baby to come. We were like two thieves plotting a bank robbery, huddled in discussion and plans for the future. For a time, April and I returned to being our former sister-self's once more. So when she boarded a train back to Wisconsin without so much as a goodbye, I was beside myself.

By my fourteenth birthday, I had made a habit of sulking in my room. Against my protests, my mother forced a cake in front of me, all the while coaxing me into celebrating. I wanted nothing more than to return to my room and allow my brain and heart to become numb. The familiar loneliness reached back in and grabbed me. I worked up the courage to confide in my mother that my sadness no longer felt like sadness, but depression.

"Um, Mom, are you busy?" I asked cautiously.

"No, I'm just going over the bills," she replied without looking up from her calculator.

I sat down next to her at the kitchen table and searched for the right phrase to express myself.

"I don't feel very happy here. Actually, I feel really depressed," I started to explain.

"Harmonie, I just don't have time for this!" She said as she pushed herself away from the table and grabbed a cigarette from the counter.

"It's always something with you kids! So what. You're depressed. Well, aren't we all!" she sneered as she took a drag and blew the smoke out in a huff. "You think you've got problems, little girl? You don't have anything to be depressed about," she stated matter-of-factly. "I don't know what to tell you. It's all in your head, so talk yourself out of it." She sat back down and redirected her attention to the notepad.

Feeling worse than before, I quietly pushed the chair away and retreated to my room. What had I expected her to say? After all, she had no time for a depressed teenage daughter when her other teen daughter was pregnant, hundreds of miles away, and her son was in prison. Meanwhile, she had a thriving toddler that needed tending to and a new marriage to settle into.

I felt like I was in the middle of nowhere screaming for help, but no one could hear me. I was raised with the "get over it, people have it worse than you" adage. Tears were weakness and lives were private, and you kept both to yourself. I couldn't take it anymore! The cans of beer under my bed went unnoticed and did little to quench my broken heart. April rarely called, and when she did, she'd only speak to my mother.

I can't recall what the date was, only that I didn't return home from school. I slept where I could and found friends who were little more than enemies. Three days after I abruptly left home, David spotted me. He charged after me through the mounds of winter snow, yelling out my name. There's no quick way to run in snow, so I did my best to trudge through the heaps. Picking up my pace I turned the corner and headed for a shoveled walkway of a random house. Just as my feet landed on the pavement, I realized it was a solid sheet of ice! I caught my balance and like a speed skater who could see the finish line, I slid past the patio doors and the strangers who looked up from their dinner to see me; arms out, feet planted on the ice, gliding by. I rounded the opposite corner and peered up the hill to see David's truck. The steam rolled out of the exhaust and the driver's door stood ajar. He headed toward his waiting vehicle, huffing and cursing at the daughter he chose to be a father to. As an adult, I laugh at that moment. It must have been a sight to see as an unsuspecting bystander. It also solidified just how much David truly cared for me.

The following night I wandered through town until it became too cold to walk the icy streets in just my jeans and the coat that I'd fled with. I had run out of places to shelter myself. With nowhere else to go, I called my mother and braced myself for the yelling I was sure to be met with.

"Why did you call so late? I just got out of the shower, and you know how I don't like to go out in the cold with wet hair," she stated calmly.

We drove in silence back to the house on the side of the mountain where deer and moose and wildcats frequented the field that sprawled out beside the long gravel driveway. I opened the front door to smells of home and the wood fireplace blazing in flames of warmth. I retreated to my room once again. I had accomplished little, aside from a monthlong grounding. I couldn't explain why I'd gone, only that I needed to. I lacked the insight to understand my true motivation. It was not my rebellion that drove me to run away, but a deep ache in my soul I tried to flee from.

April returned that spring with her newborn in tow. I quickly went from a new big sister to an aunt in less than two years and I was thrilled at both of my adjoining roles. Unlike Zach, who was a calm and happy child, Justin was a crier. He needed endless holding and was never quite content. This became even more of a problem when that summer we left the house on the side of the mountain, only to return to the small and cramped truck camper at the familiar campground on the outskirts of town.

Now instead of one baby, there were two. Instead of one new mom, there were two and they locked horns on most everything. April was learning to be a mom and my mom was endlessly mothering everyone. It wasn't long until we moved from the campground to a plot of land where my parents dreamed of building a home. Thankfully, that dream was abandoned and so was the truck camper!

Before the start of my freshman year, the five of us painted new walls and unpacked familiar items we'd forgotten about. To me, moving was a bit like Christmas. A box would be opened and I'd excitedly unwrap the newspaper, revealing the old item, that was new once more. Those little trinkets made my room mine and transformed an ordinary house into my home.

If I had to choose a favorite house, it might have been that one. I'm especially fond of it because it may have been the first time I truly felt happiness, but mostly because of the indoor pool. The house itself was a peculiar rectangle. Two bedrooms were on one side, separated by the kitchen, dining and living room. Large windows lined the back wall and looked into the massive room that housed the pool. The remaining bedroom was at the opposite end of the house, which my parents shared with Zach.

It was more than I could have hoped for. Endless acres of enormous mountain pines were in every direction and I found myself spending more time outside, even when the snow would pile up as tall as the car doors. I remember the trickle of the stream that ran parallel between the house and the field full of crisp grass. Sometimes I'd sit for hours, lost in the dreams of a teenage girl.

Under the deep blue sky, my best friend from high school and I would lay in the field and take selfies, long before anyone ever coined the phrase. We'd capture ourselves with the sun in our eyes, which made most of the photos look as though we'd been weeping from some tragedy, followed by loud laughter; the only thing that could be heard for miles.

It was peaceful there, despite April and her newborn taking up occupancy in the adjoining bedroom. She worked nights, and Justin suffered for months with colic. I'd sleepily tiptoe into their room and draw him out of his cradle. In the black of night, I'd hold him close, patting his back and quietly singing the newest Mariah Carey song until we both drifted off to sleep. Then the alarm would ring at five a.m., and I'd shuffle to the kitchen to start a pot of coffee.

I had realized, even at fourteen, that the hot liquid was necessary if I planned to stay awake through school with enough energy to make it through the evening's homework. Quietly I'd tiptoe into my parents' room and whisper to David that the coffee was ready. It was my effort at coaxing him out of bed in the wee hours. Sometimes, I still think of those mornings. Just him and me on the twenty-minute drive to where I could catch the bus to my new school, still another forty-five minutes away. We never talked much, but listened to the latest country song, which paired well with the two-lane highway and the quiet of the mountains.

Although the journey to school was long, it was a refreshing escape from the almost life-ending bullying I endured when we lived in the house on the side of the mountain. Long ago I made peace with always being the new kid in town, but had never been met with such hatred until we moved to Sandpoint, Idaho. The kids who pretended to be my friends had a secret agenda, which was to lead me into never ending traps to get beaten. I feared going to school. They were relentless, and in my young mind I couldn't fathom the crime I committed that warranted such disgust from my peers.

On an early spring day, I was met with smiles from former friends and current enemies. I remember wondering what had changed. Maybe I'd pleased them today. I wore the right clothes, said the right thing or finally they had made peace with my presence. Maybe it was the hint of warmth to come. A long frigid winter was ending and surly this made my classmates happy. Before the last bell rang, I was warned by a former friend that I should get a ride home from school.

I thought it odd, but the closer it came to the end of the day, the more it seemed their early morning smiles had returned to sneers. The final bell rang out and I watched as droves of my classmates ran outside. However they weren't waiting on the bus, they were in the courtyard. I wondered what everyone was so eagerly awaiting. Then as I turned from my locker, a boy stopped me.

"I hope you're getting a ride home because there's two hundred kids outside waiting to take their turn beating the shit out of you," he stated before he too, exited and headed for the courtyard.

My heart sank and my hands began to shake. I had nowhere to hide. I tried to gulp down the fear pulsing its way up my throat. I quickly walked down the main hallway to the doors farthest away from the courtyard. From that vantage point I was able to see out and hoped that I wouldn't be spotted. I hurried to the phone and grabbed the receiver. The cord was just long enough that I could crouch down and partially conceal myself under the shelf the payphone sat atop. I pushed the numbers into the keypad and peered out through the window to the courtyard. Sure enough, a crowd had gathered! I felt my head swirling and my heart began to pound in my ears. Ringing, ringing, ringing . . .

"Mom, pick up!" I whispered to myself.

"Hello?"

"I need you to come get me right now!" I managed to say with a shaky voice.

She didn't ask any questions. She knew about the kids at school and had met with the principal and guidance counselor several times to try to resolve the problem. This seemed to only make matters worse. My classmates became more cunning and found inventive ways to torture me. We lived just ten minutes away, but those minutes felt as though time was standing still. Every noise in the hallway sent me into a panic, and when she finally arrived, I wondered if my knees would buckle before I made it to her car.

After that, my mother agreed to homeschool me. For the remainder of eighth grade, she created homework assignments and lesson plans, all while tending to Zach. That summer we moved to the house with the pool. This time I was thankful for the move, even if it did mean having to make the long journey to a different school In the next county over.

I had come to learn that all good things ended and before I was able to finish out my freshman year, my parents announced that we were leaving Idaho. To say I was devastated would not be an accurate description. I'd only just begun to know happiness.

By most standards I was thriving. David's last name provided me with anonymity that concealed me from my father finding us and released me from the fear that he would show up and pretend to be a lawyer or officer, as he'd done in the past. I'd also fallen madly in love for the first time! I couldn't imagine being happy without him and my best friend. This time, I begged that I be allowed to finish the school year with just two months left. But the truck was loaded up with our belongings and we headed back down the winding mountain roads in which we had come.

The Charming House

Victorian homes are often referred to as charming. It's not so much their asymmetrical appearance or steeply pitched roofs and wrap around porches, it's the inside, the old-world style, that gives way to their charm. Outside of the city, down a two-lane road and two right hand turns later was a dead-end and on top of a steep driveway sat the most charming house.

Although not a Victorian, the balance of colors and light welcomed you in. Large windows overlooked an endless Dakota sky with sweeping views of the black hills that were both shaded and illuminated by the sun. The staircase leading up was a dark oak with intricate wooden spindles that Zach would later get his head stuck in. The kitchen was painted in a dark hunter green along with wallpaper that was outdated by at least ten years. It didn't take

away from the quaintness of the room and was the

entryway to my favorite part of the house: the

basement!

The stairs and landing were carpeted in a warm tan

that was so lush, I could see my footprints behind

me. A long-forgotten phone from the 1930s adorned

the wall, and although I was well into my teens, I'm

not ashamed to admit to pretending to make calls

every now and again. The basement was split into

four separate corridors, with my room being the

first. There were no ornate paintings intricately

drawn out by my mother, but I loved it all the same.

The door to my room was a thick walnut that looked

like it had hung on a sturdy barn years before. It was

a heavy door and nearly soundproof. Perfect for a

teenager with dreams of being a singersongwriter.

The room opposite mine contained a long work

bench with plenty of counter space, complete with

built in vices. I learned quite a bit while taking

woodshop class in Wisconsin. From making wooden

toy trucks to mechanically sound gumball machines,

I loved the smell of freshly sawed wood or the aroma

of the burn from etching a design into a plank of

oak. The entire room seemed fit for any project I

could have dreamt of, but the best thing about the

work room is that it housed a secret.

Upon entering the room, to the untrained eye, the

secret would have gone unnoticed. You would need

to wander to the back of the room and rotate slightly

in and around the underside of the staircase before

you'd find the mystery tucked away in the far back.

It was a simple bedroom or reading room, a space of

solitude that sat empty with a small window and

light wood paneling. A quiet room away from the

world. A room later to be occupied by my high

school boyfriend from Idaho.

My mornings began with David calling from the top

of the stairs that it was time to get up for school. He

was much too wise to make the trek down to my

room and get anywhere near my flailing arms,

resulting in waking me from my slumber. Of course I

had an alarm, which I chose not to set. I'd just begun

attending my third high school and was positive that

school was not an option I wanted to pursue. After

initially moving to a town forty-five minutes away

from the charming house, I managed to finish out

my freshmen year and make lots of friends. But we

were not destined to stay there.

David had a long drive to Rapid City for work and he

and my mom both agreed that it was easier for them

to relocate, despite the repercussions for their

daughter.

Just after my sophomore year began, my mom announced that she was having surgery. The double bed was set up in the living room where she could avoid the added physical requirement of climbing the stairs. Since April and Justin were finally in their own apartment, it was my duty to stay home and tend to my mom and four-year-old Zach. After nearly a month of playing nurse and babysitter, I returned to school.

By this point, I had resigned myself from putting out any effort at trying to fit in at yet another new school, with new faces and new teachers, who could not recall my name. I was well behind in my studies between the extended absence and the transition between high schools. I exasperated myself in typing class but was notified by the teacher that I was too far behind to catch up. In another class, a teacher expected the makeup work to be done by the end of the week. Overwhelmed, I thumbed through the assignments, paired with the others from the collective eight periods that created my school day. I'd never been a straight A student, but I managed to maintain an above-average GPA, which I thought to be acceptable.

By the time the midday bell rang, my heart felt heavy with defeat. As I made my way to my locker, a girl knocked the books out of my hands and accused me of looking at her boyfriend. I denied it, as I didn't know him, nor did I care to look at any boy while my heart pined for the boyfriend I'd left behind in Idaho. I challenged her to a fight, right then and there. After the bullying I had already endured, I abandoned any fear of physical pain. In the summer after eighth grade, I decided that I'd much rather stand my ground than quiver at the fear of fists. I'd gone through the worst I could imagine where bullying was concerned, and I wasn't about to stand down now.

When I began high school, I made a promise to myself that I wouldn't cower to those who were too young and ignorant to understand how irrelevant I was in the grand scheme of life. The alpha and omega of teen drama no longer concerned me. I wasn't interested in becoming their muse of anguish. I learned that my words could be more powerful than their threats. My sarcasm forthright yet hidden in the words they only knew existed in a dictionary. It was my armor and my defense. I also learned that sticking up for yourself and for the underdog was often worth the temporary pain of getting punched in the face.

Exasperated by the demanding workload and the incident with the girl, any remaining energy I began the day with quickly dissipated. Once again I called my mom from the school payphone. When she arrived, I was sitting atop the brick sign that displayed my school's name, a cigarette in hand, and a look on my face that told her not to question the decision she already knew I made. I would not return to school again. It was my last and seventeenth school I attended.

David wasted no time in making me get a job. He said if I wasn't learning, then I was to be working. So, I got a job and worked till late in the night or early in the morning. I'd drag my tired legs down the stairs to my room with the heavy door where I'd drift off to sleep, sometimes at two or three in the morning. Then I'd be awoken at seven so that I could take care of Zach, since my mom had returned to work. After flipping on *Barney* and pretending to watch with him, I'd nap in five-minute intervals until lunch. By five, it was time to grab a quick dinner and sometimes no dinner at all. I needed to be ready when David returned from work, only to turn around and drive me to my place of employment.

The driving age in South Dakota was only fourteen, and since I was already fifteen, I hoped to receive my license. Since I no longer attended school, I wasn't able to take Driver's Education, and I had little driving experience. David decided that he would be my instructor. On my next day off from work, we climbed into the old Chevy Silverado, and he explained where the gears were.

I remember when my mom explained the same thing to April while teaching her to drive in the silver Datsun that she owned in North Carolina. Where David was patient, my mom was dramatic and would make up scenarios to test April's reactions. April would ease the car into first gear, and it'd jut forward and then stall, jerking and jawing me in the back seat. The long dusty dirt roads on the outskirts of the city were perfect for a first-time driver. The grazing cows and horses who stood like cardboard cutouts in the shamrock pastures seemed unbothered by the car's sudden movements. My mother would instruct April to ease her foot off the clutch as she eased onto the gas. Again April would put the car into gear and try once more. As she became more familiar with the dance of clutch, gas, shift, my mother would suddenly yell out, "STOP, there's a dog in the road!" April would slam on the brakes to avoid hitting the imaginary animal as I braced myself against the headrest.

During the long journey from Idaho to South Dakota, April and my mom would take turns driving. I'd watch as they played driver change at the roadside rest stops. Seats were arranged, mirrors adjusted, and seat belts were fastened before we headed off again. As April began to enter the highway from the ramp, my mom would instruct her to "MERGE, MERGE, MERGE!" Sometimes when I'm tired and I'm well below travel speeds as I'm entering the highway, I still hear my mom shouting and her voice ringing in my head.

I caught on to the shifting pretty quick, but struggled on hills, as most new drivers do. On the highways and side streets, I'd smile as I grabbed the stick on the side of the column, remembering what David taught me. The Datsun had been a "four on the floor," the Chevy was a "three in the tree." He sat on the passenger side of the long bench seat and watched intently. He didn't give me false praise or much praise at all, but I easily knew when he was pleased. When, without having to be instructed, I knew when to shift between the gears, he'd ease back in the seat and gaze out the window or flip on the radio, as though we were simply out for an

afternoon drive.

We rounded through the large neighborhood and

past the black hills that were cast in shadows of

rolling clouds. I eased to a stop and diligently

checked for traffic. I spotted a long clearing and

flung the stick into first gear. Although I'd mastered

taking off, the pull of the hill rolled me back. I

released the clutch and the truck stalled out. Again I

tried, but the result was the same. Now David sat

forward from the seat and eyed the oncoming traffic.

No words of encouragement were given, only that I

would need to quickly move the foot pedals in order

to avoid killing the engine again.

I took a breath and waited for my chance. With his

advice in mind, I quickly hit the gas as my left foot

leapt off the clutch and with a long screech of the

tires, I turned the wheel and we were out on the

highway! I surprised and scared myself at the same time with what seemed to be a reckless move. I turned to David to gauge his reaction, but he burst into a roar of laughter! "That was fun!" he said. "I think you got it." We laughed all the way home.

South Dakota was different from all of the other places I'd lived, not only aesthetically, but there was a mood there. Maybe it was in the people I met through the youth center or the older peers who hung out at The Atomic Café, a coffee house by day and rave party by night. Nevertheless, I was intrigued with this new diversity. From the barista who easily could have passed for Patrick Swayze's twin brother to the guy with the tallest mohawk that, still, to this day, I've ever seen. From gay to straight, from Native American to black, it was no matter; all were accepted. There was no expectation to fit in, but to be whoever you were and no one else.

Through the many moves, I crafted a unique talent of becoming a chameleon. As I sat in observation and watched interactions, I could gauge who might be an ally and which group would be an enemy. The survival technique was imperative when breaking into cliques at school. It was a method of survival. I hadn't known the freedom to be who I was until now and they embraced me as if I always belonged.

For the first time, I felt like I found home. Was it this place or the person I was becoming? Had I changed and found within myself a resolution that home could be wherever your heart is at peace? I'd never known much of it, nor had I known to search for it. Among the hills and history that told of the many who struggled to come here in pursuit of a better life, I found that I too had been changed by the rugged landscape.

While I embraced my new life, I hadn't forgotten about my lost love. I dated others, but my heart still broke for him. Those first love feelings are hard to shake, especially when they're abruptly driven hundreds of miles away. We continued to write and call one another. Then my best friend called to tell me that she was coming to visit with her boyfriend and my lost love, John. I was beside myself. My love for him hadn't changed, but I was nervous to see him. Would it be the same or would it feel as if too much time had passed, I wondered. Then came the moment we were together once more and my heart leapt back into his and his into mine.

After several days it became clear that she and her boyfriend overstayed their welcome and my mom insisted that I tell them to go. But John could not return. He had been abandoned by his family and had no real place to return to. April offered her couch and then he and I were together again for a time, in love for the moment. The two of us had fought to stay together and saw no other choice than to hold on to one another. Aside from our minimumwage jobs and knowing that we wanted to get married when we were legally old enough to agree, there were no thoughts of the future. Where we might live or what we might do for careers was undecided. All I knew for sure was that my heart

was set on becoming a singer and his heart was set on me. Being with him and in South Dakota proved that happiness was possible again.

Then suddenly, my sister kicked him out without warning. Her one bedroom was not fitted for an extra long-term guest, but what would happen to John now? How my parents concluded that the best idea was to move John into the secret room under the stairs may have been due to their distress from

April's announcement. She was pregnant for the second time. It wasn't long afterward that the living arrangement expired and John was asked to leave in order to make room for a pregnant April and little Justin.

Justin and Zach grew up like brothers. Although Zach had been born prematurely, he quickly caught up and exceeded all expectations. He would have full on conversations at two years old and was almost four feet tall by three! Justin was quiet in the talking arena, but he was a ball of energy and mischief. Where Zach became the gentle giant,

Justin was the unruly house guest. Zach would fear Justin's tantrums and in the same breath defend him against any perceived enemies. I loved them both for their own ways, their own unique personalities and traits and I was thankful to have such a full house once again. But I was not about to allow John to become the past and as young lovestruck teens do, I took it out on my parents.

My mom's solution was to allow me to go back to Idaho with him. So, I chose leave home and be with John. I packed up my things in boxes and bags as she drove us to meet a friend of his who agreed to drive us. John loaded my things in the trunk as my mom sat quietly in her car puffing her cigarette, the red glow blaring and dulling every few seconds. I glanced back at Zach several times, who was watching the exchange intently. He too loved John and true to form for Zach, he created a silly name for him, Peter. I still don't understand why Zach called him that or why he made up words that everyone seemed to immediately understand. It was Zach language and his name for me was Mimi.

When I was a little girl, I referred to myself as Mimi as well, although I parted with it when I became old enough to pronounce my name correctly. So, Zach

had no way of knowing that his name for me was

also my name for myself. As I stared back at my first

love, my baby brother and then at my first romantic

love and then to the boxes that filled the trunk, I

said my goodbyes in my head and prepared to say

them aloud when I heard Zach call out, "Mimi, don't

go!"

How could he understand the decision I was about

to make and the tear my heart was evaluating.

Which would hurt more, to leave John or leave Zach

behind? I turned to John and in his eyes, I knew he

knew. He grabbed the boxes and bags and returned

them to my mother's waiting car. After a hug and a

tearful kiss, he was gone. I returned to the

passenger side of the vehicle and opened the door.

Zach sprang to the front seat and wrapped his arms

around my neck. I remember the softness of his hair

and the pilling of his white and red footy pajamas

that he fashioned in the late evening in preparation

for bedtime.

"Let's go home," I stated.

We drove off as I listened to Zach ramble on about

the scenery outside his window. Innocently, not

knowing that I had chosen him. In silent

contemplation, I stared out at the light rain that

created a glare from the beams of streetlights on the

wet asphalt. Did I make the right decision? I

wondered. What would have become of me in Idaho

with a teenage boyfriend and a tenth-grade

education? Yes, I resolved. I had made the right

decision, even though my heart was now separated

by two boys whom I both loved in very different

ways.

That summer, April's baby arrived. I never met the

baby and have no memory of the event. April slinked

away to the secret room where she slept for days,

only to awaken and find that she was no longer

April, but a mother who had given part of her heart

to a family whose heart was now full.

The House on the Lake

Sunsets have mystified me since as far back as I can

recall. To me there is nothing more beautiful than

watching the sun being swallowed by a body of

water. It's as though it's melting, sliver by sliver and

with it, its beams mix with the water to form

magentas and paisley pinks or glorious reds,

twisting into brilliant oranges and swirling into

night.

I'd always wanted to live on a lake. Not just near a

lake, but right there next to it. I imagined wading

into the water each morning and the glorious

sunsets at dusk. After two short stints of living in month-to-month apartments, we moved into a remodeled vacation home that sat on a small lake.

Although winter had begun, I would bundle myself with scarves and gloves and grab my song writing notebook and head out to the edge of the water. For cumbersome writing, a poet or lyricist could not ask for better, as most days were much too cold to enjoy and I was hard pressed to find a spot of sun through the gray fluffy clouds.

My writing was my escape and an outlet for my emotions. Although I sang often, my stage fright persisted. Eight years in choir did nothing to curb this. In choir I excelled and sang as if no one could see or hear me. But in front of others, when I received full attention, my voice quivered, and my notes would shake. Despite my soprano voice that showcased Latin opera and could shift to an Etta

James blues without hesitation, I lacked trust in my talent.

In her quest to help cure my stage fright, my mom persuaded me to audition at the mall for a modeling agency called The Trendsetters. I had no problems with public speaking and certainly not walking a runway. Singing and song writing was a special part of who I was, and because of this, it caused me to be self-critical. But I was willing to audition if there was a possibility that I could overcome my fear. If nothing else, it would make my mother happy.

I remember seeing many young women at the mall of various ages, from mid-teens to midtwenties, who anxiously waited for their number to be called. We were instructed to climb the three steps and walk to the end of the runway, state our name and our age, then walk back and depart the stage. My number was somewhere in the middle. I waited long enough that I was able to watch some of the other girls walk, some fumbling or stomping down the long stretch of carpeted stage and others who seemed well practiced. At the end of the stage, they'd announce themselves. Some were so quiet that I didn't know if they ever managed to state their name and others so loud, they sounded as though they were announcing the score at a baseball game.

My turn came and I confidently walked down the runway. My body hadn't changed much since junior high; however, I abandoned the dirty dishwater hair for a golden blond dye job. I had long thick locks that flowed down to the middle of my back and crystal blue eyes that were often described as aquamarine. Now I stood at the end of the runway. I stated my name and age clearly and was met with a sea of smiles from the judges and nods from the audience. I had no expectation of becoming part of this elite modeling team and no real aspiration to become a model. My flippant attitude matched my sarcasm and my "take it or leave it" philosophy. Yet I trusted my mother; and if she thought this would help build my singing confidence, I was willing to give it a try.

When the time came for the numbers to be called, I was fourth on the list. I wasn't exactly sure what this meant, but I was congratulated and welcomed as a model to The Trendsetters. We would soon be preparing for our first show and would need to work on our runway walk. Week after week I worked my stance, walking back and forth through the kitchen when no one was watching. I learned arm placement and to keep my head up and when to smile (and when not to smile).

A month later it was time for the show. I was backstage with the models, and chaos had ensued.

Who was to wear which dress? Who was next in line to have hair and makeup done? Where were the shoes for the thin model with the perfect forehead? The agency's owner came into the dressing area only to find me announcing orders and doling out dresses one by one. She grabbed my arm, pulling me up from the floor and breaking my concentration.

"Why aren't you dressed?" she inquired.

"I was helping the other girls get ready," I responded with a shrug.

"How did you figure out the order of the models and the dresses they were to wear?"

I went on to explain myself as she stood there, befuddled. What came next surprised me. She asked if I minded sitting out the show to help with the models. I was honored, of course, that she had confidence in my ability and trusted me with the task, so I agreed.

After the show, she offered me a job as her liaison. I didn't feel a loss over not modeling in the shows. Becoming her liaison meant more to me. She saw talents in me I had not yet been able to see in myself. The experience never did cure my stage fright but taught me the invaluable: the value of myself and in following my instincts. Sometimes one opportunity might lead you someplace you'd never imagine for yourself. I was later recruited by a top modeling agency, but at five-three, the jobs would consist of car modeling, and I couldn't stand the thought of hanging on a calendar in a slimy bathroom. So with that, my modeling career ended, but my thirst for being an entrepreneur had just begun.

I continued with my full-time job and full-time responsibilities, which included paying my parents rent. I was also responsible for buying my own toiletries and many times my own food. Yet I was still expected to succumb to their rules and help tend to Zach. Friends were hard to come by since I didn't have much time to make them and we lived miles outside of town. Without additional money to purchase a car of my own, I was stuck in the monotony of work and home. I grew resentful and was quick to lose my temper with my mom, whom I saw as a hindrance to my happiness. So, when we got in a squabble over something I cannot recall, she delivered her infamous line that changed the course of my life forever. In the midst of our argument about the thing I don't remember, she said "Well if you don't like it, leave!"

"I will then. I'll move out!" I yelled at her.

"You're never going to find someone to rent to a seventeen-year-old, little girl!" She sneered.

I was a stubborn young woman and learned throughout my childhood how to be resourceful. If there was a will then I would surely find a way and I usually did! I opened the newspaper and saw an ad for a job that offered an apartment above the shop. When I called, an older woman answered and asked me several questions. After I satisfied her quarries, she informed me that I would need to start in just a few weeks.

I hung up the phone and spun around with a wide smile on my face. My mom was standing behind me. I smugly announced that I had indeed found someone to rent an apartment to me and that I would be leaving at the beginning of the following month. The next few weeks were a pleasant time at home. I dreamed of a new life where the rent I paid would be rewarded with my freedom, and the food I purchased would be mine to eat.

I gave my notice at the retail store and soon I was in the car accompanied by my mom, David and Zach. The hour and a half drive to the boat dock was lively as my mom reminded me to use the brain that God gave me and to be safe and that she loved me. I knew all of this already, but I smiled and nodded and reminded her that I loved her as well.

I arrived on Mackinac Island with a suitcase and a couple boxes of belongings. The lilacs were in full bloom, with beautiful purples and rosy pinks that assaulted my allergies as I collected my items from the ferry. The island bustled with visitors in horsedrawn carriages and workers who whizzed past me on bikes. I loaded my belongings onto a hand cart and made my way down the street. The shop's doors stood wide open, welcoming patrons to come in for a closer look. I quickly understood what drew so many tourists to the place that was lost in time.

However, I wasn't sure how I would be able to get past the sweet smell of lilacs and decadent fudge, mixed with the wafting smell of horse shit.

The retail shop was located in a quaint building, painted in simple white with a faux upper deck that outlined the window of the apartments. The door on the side of the building gave way to a long staircase that led to the upper floor. I dragged my suitcase through the corridor and past the simple kitchen on the right. Then I arrived at the last door. The door that opened into my apartment. It consisted of two double beds and one large dresser, as well as a private en suite. The two front windows looked down onto the street below that was lined with shops full of T-shirts and trinkets, as well as what turned out to be a very lively bar. I had no roommate and was thankful for this. It was my very own place and I felt exhilarated knowing that I was on my own.

I carefully unpacked and placed my items in familiar locations before making my way to the shop and introducing myself to my new employer.

Mrs. Smith was a heavy-set woman, who wore old sweatshirts and was recently single after her husband left her for another woman who was half her age. She was forthright with her bitterness and made it clear that she wasn't interested in her employees fraternizing outside of their work. Her daughter Audra was old enough to be my mother and was the watchdog when the old lady was away. They lived on the island their entire lives and had done quite well at running the shop and tending to their employees, while also keeping a watchful eye on their resident's habits.

The nights were loud, filled with tourists and workers alike. I would lie in bed in the late-night hours, willing them to quiet before the six o'clock morning shined onto my pillow and nudged me awake for my shift. Yelling "shut up" from the window didn't seem to put a damper on their party mood. I'd huff my way back over to bed and throw the pillow over my ear.

I didn't mind working at the shop, ringing up customers and folding the endless Mackinac Island gimmick shirts. It allowed my mind the free time it needed to daydream and craft songs that I filled my notebook with in the evening. Leading into my second week on the island, I again snuggled in bed and listened to the bar across the street push out people from last call. I decided that I had had enough! How was I to sleep with the constant noise?!

So, on the fourteenth night, instead of washing my face and brushing my teeth and crawling into bed to stare at the blank wall, I took a shower and put on fresh makeup and my favorite pair of jeans and I exited the stairwell on the side of the shop. I picked a direction and started my stroll, taking in the music and laughter inside the late-night establishments. There was a buzz inside me and an invigoration that I hadn't felt before. I reached the end of the sidewalk as the street opened up to a view of the glimmering lake and the sprawling green lawn that ran up the hillside.

The once lively sounds of downtown faded into the background. I could hear the gentle waves lapping against the boats that rocked against the pier. Some people were meandering near the water, but one young man was sitting in the park. I approached and introduced myself. I always found it easier to make friends with the opposite sex. I was easily annoyed by the endless drama that most girls revolved around and found that I much rather talk about old cars than about the latest fashion. He and I spent the rest of the night talking and walking the streets of the island. That was also the night that ended my eleven p.m. bedtime.

I loved the island and the overall vibe of the people who were there finding out who they were. Some like me, experiencing for the first time being on their own. I'd call my family and tell them all that I missed them, and I did miss them. I'd call April and Bryan and tell them of the latest friend I made or the new experiences I had. April and Justin even came to visit me once. I spent the day showing them around and introducing April to my new best friend, Genni.

Genni and I met at the top of one of the many hills on the Island, not long after I sailed across Lake Huron and while I was still learning all of the secrets the island had in store for me. It was the first warm day of the season and my day off from the shop. I walked alone with excitement and intrigue at all there was to explore. I had no real direction, although I heard arch rock was a beautiful view and that on a clear day, you could see across the lake to Canada. I loved stopping to smell the many varieties of flowers and decided to pick one and carry it home. Just as I plucked the alluring violet bud from the tree, I heard a voice ring out.

"You're NOT supposed to pick the flowers!"

I turned to see a pretty teen with curly red hair and a face full of freckles.

"You're not supposed to pick the flowers," she repeated. "It's against the law here, and they'll give you a fine," she explained.

"Oh, I didn't know that. I'm Harmonie," I stated.

"You looked like my friend from last season, but you're not," she replied with an attitude and accent I recognized.

"So, what's your name?" I inquired.

"Genni," she responded curtly. She began to walk, and I matched her pace, excited at the potential of yet another new friend, even if she did appear a bit stuck up.

"This must be your first season," she stated.

"Yes. I guess you were here last year?" I asked.

"Yea, this is my second season. I work at the shop next to Watersmeet."

Watersmeet was the bar that was across from my apartment, which meant that she worked directly across the street from me!! We spent the rest of the day walking and talking. Later we'd say that she was the snob and that I was the one who talked too much and probably both descriptions were true. As it turned out, when the season was over, she'd return home to Wisconsin. We discussed our plans to go to the line dancing event that was taking place that weekend. As some young women do, we had a mutual frenemy and bonded over our dislike for the girl.

After that, Genni and I were inseparable. We planned our days off from work together and would take the ferry to the mainland and shop or have lunch at a little Chinese restaurant which made the best pu pu platter either of us ever had! When we were at work, I'd often look over to find her in the doorway of her shop, pointing to her watch to announce she wanted to take a break. So, we'd have lunch together and take breaks together and we became as close as two girls could be without any sexual intentions. Because of this we both had landed on the same word from the same article we had read at different times, unbeknownst to the other: *agapē*, unconditional love without sexual intent. From then on out, we would say, "I agapē you!" We'd depart. "See you tomorrow. I agapē you!" And we did.

Among the many friends I made on the island, no one was like Genni or could ever be. We liked to sit on the dock and dangle our legs over the water. She'd listen to a playlist of songs I'd sing and was my most captivated audience of my own lyrics, where she too could hear the melody of the song in my head.

We once blew up inner tubes and decided we could float the nine miles around the island. After an hour of waves pushing us back toward shore and tired arms, we finally fled the idea and walked the block and a half back to the small beach we had set sail from. Genni was a little less than two years older than me, but this meant that she was old enough to enter the watering holes that I was just one year shy of. If I wasn't granted permission to enter by the doorman, then she would turn away and tell me she'd rather hang out with me anyway. We never failed to find our own fun anyways. If it wasn't stealing a tandem bike from a naive tourist and swiftly getting pulled over by a bicycle cop, then it was finding our way onto a yacht during the boat races that led from Chicago to the island and back again. We set sail with men from Canada and then returned to retell our stories of the "shekies" who took us for a ride.

Our adventures together led us back to the mainland, where one particular day we took a taxi to a town about a half hour south. We entered a

tattoo shop, and I picked a small hummingbird to be

inked into my sun-kissed thigh. When I was asked

for my ID, I opened my bag and pretended to

rummage through. My acting skills spilled out as I

looked with a panicked face at Genni and the young

man behind the counter.

"Oh shit! I think I left it on the island. Shit, shit, shit!"

I exclaimed with dismay.

"I can't believe you forgot it!" Genni chimed in.

The unsuspecting man behind the counter looked

from me to Genni.

"What's your zodiac sign?" he asked.

"Aquarius," I stated with a bit of confusion.

"Well, okay then, I believe you. Come on back and

we'll get that tattoo started!"

Genni sat on the stool facing me. She'd already experienced her first tattoo the previous year—a pretty green frog placed between her shoulder blades. In the cab ride I'd asked her if it had hurt, and she confidently told me no, so I wasn't fearful that my thigh was in any harm. The tattoo artist got to work, and Genni and I joked and talked while the ink gun buzzed along. Twenty minutes later it was done!

"Wow, you were right, that didn't hurt at all!" I told her.

"Really? Mine hurt like a son of a bitch!" she said with a smile. I laughed and gave her a playful smack on the arm.

I paid the man my money and asked him one departing question.

"Just curious, why did you ask what my zodiac is?"

"Because if you were lying about your age, you wouldn't know your zodiac." Genni and I laughed about that and the entire ordeal for years to come.

There was no shortage of parties or of potential mates on Mackinac, and in no time I met a cute boy who quickly became my boyfriend. He would bring me raspberry steamers while I worked, despite Mrs. Smith running him off. There were no visitors allowed in my apartment, as was the case with the majority of residences on the island. So when I had overslept one morning, Mrs. Smith used her key to open my door, only to find him occupying the tiny bed with me fully naked, wrapped in his embrace. His free spirit matched mine perfectly, and we'd hop from party to party, with one of us secretly sneaking into the other's apartment to pass out for the night.

Other times I'd drink my way to oblivion and stumble home with two hours to spare before my shift started. With the many late nights, the drinking and the beckoning from my friends to go out, I became sick with exhaustion. I thumbed a ride back to my parents' home for a much-needed visit and a room that was quiet by eleven p.m. I slept and hugged Zach and caught my mom up on my friends and the day-to-day nuances of island life. I showed off my new tattoo and to my delight, my mother happily smiled and commented on the cuteness of it all. On the third night, I dreamed my boyfriend cheated on me and the next morning I begged my mother to drive me to the ferry.

When I arrived, many friends approached and asked me if I knew what happened while I was away. I looked for him in all of the usual places, then finally waited for night. I knew he'd be working in the kitchen of the bar where I'd been removed from many times. They knew I was underage, but on slow nights they would humor me by allowing me to dance with my friends. It was only on the nights where I'd spend hours owning the pool table, winning game after game and hand over fist, that a sore loser would complain. Then I would be made to leave under the premise that I was an illegal minor.

I made my way to the pub where I confirmed my dream. He'd confessed his feelings for me the night before I returned home but found himself with someone else the following day. It didn't help that I still loved John and was far from being over him. I missed him deeply and longed to have that romantic love again. Although I wasn't in love with this boy, it didn't mean that the betrayal hurt any less.

I wanted to be happy on the island and at times I was. Still, there was a hole inside me: an ache that I couldn't make sense of. From an early age, alcohol allowed me to numb myself. However temporary it was, it became a reprieve from my inner turmoil that I hid within lyrics and deep inside me. I filled my time with the occasional casual encounter with men who spent their vacations on the island and forgot them as quickly as they boarded the departing ferry.

Things for me were unraveling, and the partying led to more experiences with smoking pot, although I never quite enjoyed it. If I wasn't suffering from paranoia and cottonmouth, I was catatonic and unable to convey the itch of the rash on my body that I was also unable to scratch. Despite my allergy to the magic of marijuana, I continued to mix large blunts with a multitude of hard alcohol and forties.

The partying and heartache led me to the island's drug dealer's house at the top of a steep hill. It was past the Grand Hotel, where tourists had no business exploring. Few were capable of walking the vertical incline without the assistance of a carriage,

pulled by one of the many horses that trotted past

us that night. Genni and another friend

accompanied me to the house to procure some weed

that was rumored to be the best on the island. I sat

on the far end of the couch, closest to the door,

leaving plenty of distance between me and the drug

dealer. Genni and our other friend sat caddy-corner

on the other sofa. Pink Floyd's *The Wall* was playing,

which I reveled in. "Comfortably Numb" had been

my anthem since first hearing it as a young girl. I'd

lie on my bed staring at the ceiling, listening to its

lyrics on repeat and finding comfort that a

songwriter conveyed so perfectly the feeling inside

me.

The blunts were passed, and the forties were

guzzled. Now, looking back, I cannot understand

how I was able to consume copious amounts of

alcohol and live to tell the tale. At just seventeen I'd

blacked out twice before. I used the bitter ale to stop

the intruding thoughts of things I could not change,

and this night proved to be no different, but yet it

was. With the alcohol coursing through my

bloodstream and the catatonia of the weed, I sat

motionless, unable to do more than observe the

evening through my glazed eyes.

Genni made several attempts at getting a taxi, but to

no avail. One had promised to be there within

minutes, but after an hour, she and the other girl

resolved to make the long walk back to their

respective apartments. The horses must have grown

tired that night, and so no one would arrive to save

me from the event that would occur. I remember

watching them depart through the front door. The

innocence of leaving their friend at a boy's house

who appeared harmless by any standard. It

happened to be the last thing I would remember.

The next morning, I awoke naked in a bed I didn't

recognize with a boy that I did. A flash of him on top

of me, and then nothing else but black. I begged my

brain to remember, but the only thing I could grasp

was the door closing behind my friends and the

music of *The Wall*. How had I gotten here in this bed,

with this person? I slowly rose to sit and felt the

familiar feeling inside me. The feeling of someone

having been inside me. In my stupor, I racked my

brain again. I could not remember a kiss, nor a no

and not a yes. I quickly dressed as he awoke. I

remember looking at him and my stomach churning.

I can still taste the burn of the alcohol mixed with

the stomach acid that rose in the back of my throat.

"I've got to go home," I stammered.

"Okay, I'll walk you," he said.

I didn't want to be walked home by him! I tied my shoes and tried my best to get to the door before he had a chance to throw on his old and dirty pair of jeans and white tank top. My mind was fogged by too much alcohol and weed from the night before, and I moved in slow motion. So slowly that he matched my steps and we exited together. My regrets burned inside me for being too stoned to move through that same door the night before. As he walked next to me, he put his arm around my shoulders, and I shivered with disgust.

"So, I guess we're going out now," he stated with confidence.

My suspicion was confirmed. What I feared had happened while I was too obliterated to consent to was true. I shoved his arm away and ran down the steep hill to my apartment. I showered in the hottest water my skin would endure and then sat in a towel

at the edge of my bed.

I stared at myself in the full-length mirror that hung

on the outside of the bathroom door. I appeared no

different in my reflection than I had the previous

night. There was no alarming transformation or any

telltale sign that would announce to an

unsuspecting onlooker what had occurred. As I

looked into my own eyes, I concluded that this is

what happens to a stupid girl that drinks too much

and smokes her broken heart into a state where her

body will not respond to the begging inside her

brain and her lips cannot say no.

I dressed and made my way to the shop for the long

day ahead. I would go on to blame myself for the

next twenty-five years. I blamed myself because I

knew better or at least I should have known better. I

had no business being there. I had no business

drinking or smoking, and what happened was a

lesson in stupidity. I made a mistake and what

happened was my fault. It was a lesson to be learned

and never repeated. For the next twenty-five years I

believed this to be true, until a movement that

changed that moment for me: #MeToo.

Baby's First Home

The sunroom had windows for walls. It was illuminated from dawn until dusk. The entire room was warm and bright, and it was the only nice thing in the old building, which was nothing more than a rundown house. It was situated near the center of town and converted into two apartments. One on the bottom floor and one on the top. Ours was on the top floor. There was an enormous kitchen with a small sink where I'd stand on top of a dish towel to keep the fiberglass tiles from itching my feet. The best thing about that first apartment wasn't the sunroom, though; it was that it was mine and Genni's!

After I abruptly left Mackinac, Genni and I continued to

write. Then, just after my eighteenth birthday, she

pulled up in a rusty 1978 Chevy Caprice and hauled

me and my things back to Wisconsin with her. It

didn't last long, though. Just eight months in, we

decided to make an about-face and return to

Michigan.

The old car barely got us back across the border, but

we knew as long as we had each other, we'd be fine

wherever we ended up. My parents owned a

doublewide that sat on a couple acres of beautifully

manicured grass with a tree line full of wild berries

and deer. We happily accepted when they offered us

their basement.

I jokingly nicknamed Genni "Fire-starter" since she

had a knack for getting the small wood burner

ablaze. We'd huddle together under piles of

blankets among the cold concrete that housed us

inside the earth. Sometimes, during the harsh

winter nights, we'd sneak up to the living room. Too exhausted from the nightshift washing fiberglass parts and too cold to put together a fire, we'd lay our weary bodies down on the soft carpet and sleep until my mother would scold us and send us away. The only reprieve to the cold and monotony was the local watering hole, where we'd dance and flirt and come home giggling as though we were still two schoolgirls.

The late nights hadn't hindered me from working toward my goals. Just before moving with Genni, I obtained my GED. I hadn't prepared in any way. I was told to request the large yellow bound book from the library, and I did. I picked it up and eyed the cover. Then, I flipped through the pages as if it were a kineograph, and I half expected there to be a stick figure dancing and waving in its corners. That was the extent of my studying. From that moment, I decided to wing it!

Somehow I passed and had newfound confidence. Once I returned to Michigan, I signed up to take the ACT. I was admitted to Ferris State, where I planned to work on my music degree. But when the time came, there was no money for the dorm. There wasn't money for much of anything, so Genni and I rented a weekly motel an hour south of Grand Rapids. We pooled our money and worked day and night, returning to the bed we shared together with nothing more than agapē between us.

Through my job in sales, I met a man whom I was quite enamored with. It wasn't long until more nights were spent in his apartment than at the motel, and I quickly moved in. It also gave way to a new relationship with April. She was recently married and lived close by. It also afforded me the opportunity to play with Justin, who, by that time, was just turning five. He was full of energy and would wave to the passersby and say, "Hi, friend!" Justin is one of those people who has never met a stranger. He possesses the type of confidence that one can only be born with and it didn't hurt that he was an imp to his core. He would entertain me for hours with his big personality and sweet smile.

I rarely thought of the times from when I was a girl that broke my family and my heart. I buried that piece of me, and I left those memories, along with the memory of the boy who had raped me, on the island. I promised myself to never think of it again. I pushed those thoughts into the far back of my mind. It became much easier once I refocused my attention on the life growing inside of me.

The man who had gifted me with the little life isn't worth mentioning here, but it wasn't long until I realized that I would be on my own. I returned to the motel, and I searched my heart for the solution to my pregnancy. I was nineteen, broke, and by no means would I return to my parents' home. I weighed each option. I had heard the little heartbeat and saw the blob on the ultrasound. I couldn't find it within me to terminate it. So, I could do as I had watched my sister do and give the baby up for adoption. Certainly there was a family who pined for a child of their own.

I remember how my mom struggled with April's adoption. Then there was April, who had made the decision, but returned changed and had put the locket with the baby's picture away, so that she would not be reminded of her choice. She and I had never discussed it much. It was unimaginable for me to fully comprehend the selfless act and the hurt she must have carried with her. No, I thought, I could not make my family endure that again.

But what did *I* want? What could I provide for this child? I'd been reckless the last few years and far too immature to raise a child. In my heart I already knew the answer. I loved the life that was so tiny and new. If I was to keep this child, I had to choose something more. I had to choose to be selfless and present and to love it with everything I had. It was decided. I would keep the baby, despite the difficulties of raising it alone. I chose to become a mom.

I couldn't decide on a name. Whatever I picked, I needed to be mindful of since he'd be stuck with it his entire life. I read a plethora of baby name books and complied a long list that I reviewed often. By the time I was into my sixth month of pregnancy, I narrowed down the names by meaning: Truth,

Faithful, and a new name. I would break free of the

past and the life that came with the cursed surname,

a name to me that was associated with pain and

penalties, even if I still possessed it at his birth. He

would be free of it, and a new legacy would be born.

Kaelib was born under a bright blue sky that

masked the frigid January temperatures. The

pregnancy was difficult. I suffered from

hyperemesis gravidarum until I was eight months

pregnant. I worked second shift, and I'd stop on the

drive to work in the late afternoon and open the car

door and throw up. I couldn't even hold down a

vitamin or much of anything for that matter. I had

few cravings, but for the first time in ten years, I

couldn't get enough of mustard!

When the sickness finally subsided, I was struck

with weeks of bronchitis and heartburn. By the

middle of my eight month of pregnancy, I came into

labor only to be sent home a multitude of times. A week went by with my water leaking and the doctors reassuring me that the umbilical cord around my baby's neck was not preventing his oxygen intake. My contractions weren't timely, and I was still not dilated past one centimeter. Nowadays, they would have induced me instead of allowing me the stress of a long labor and a baby born gray from lack of oxygen.

For most new mothers, they welcome the opportunity to show off their newborns, but I found myself selfish, made worse by postpartum hormones. I would demand him back after five minutes, like a child who was forced to share her new toy. He was quiet and would coo when I held him as he slept. I'd spend hours taking pictures of him and in pure awe of his being.

Genni wasn't just my best friend, but my birth coach and Kaelib's godparent. She quickly fell in love with Kaelib, as most people did. Before Kaelib ever made it known that he had awoken in the night, Genni would sneak into my room and rescue him from his cradle. When the light poured into my room and stretched out upon my eyes, announcing that I'd slept in, I'd jolt up and rush to his crib. Then I'd hear him squealing and Genni making silly noises from the living room downstairs.

We departed the motel for the townhouse just a few months before Kaelib was born. It was a new build and a refreshing change from our first apartment. There were no itchy kitchen tiles or slanted floor that felt as though you were walking uphill in order to get to the bathroom. No, the townhouse was the perfect place for a family, regardless of how unorthodox it may have appeared to outsiders in 1998.

Genni, by most standards, was my co-parent, and we shared in the joy Kaelib brought into our home. When he was four months old, Genni burst through the door and in a sweet voice exclaimed, "HELLO!" Kaelib smiled a toothless grin and responded, "HELLOOOO!" We shouldn't have been surprised at hearing his first word so early since he'd already made it clear that he was quite advanced for his age. But we still turned to each other in amazement.

We not only shared his first words, but she and I had grown even closer. She was my closest confidante. She advocated for me when the contractions were too much and was there to cut Kaelib's umbilical cord. Through tears she held the scissors, and in that moment I knew our bond was sealed. She always reminded me that just because we had arguments, it did not mean our friendship would end. She and I rarely fought, but this was a new concept to me. With so many losses I'd already endured, she taught me the possibility of reconciliation and of forgiveness and love.

Kaelib was perfect in every way, although I am a completely biased commentator. But he was undoubtedly beautiful. I'd bundle him up in his blue fuzzy one-piece with the hood that framed his face like a famed snow baby and venture to the grocery store. Many people would approach to see the baby with the porcelain skin. One time, a woman pointed a finger and poked his cheek as he was napping in the carrier that was secured in the cart. When his eyes popped open, she jutted back with surprise! "Oh, I thought he wasn't real! I thought it was a very lifelike doll," she exclaimed. He was indeed a beautiful baby.

When Kaelib was just nine months old, Genni and I

decided to follow my family to Kentucky. I dreamed

of a new start, and once I turned twenty-one, I filed

for a petition to legally change my last name too.

Now Kaelib and I would share this name and leave

the bitter taste of the past behind.

On Our Own

I liked to say that I didn't like being a mom, but that I loved being Kaelib's mom. He filled my heart with a love I hadn't known existed. I rarely displayed anger at Kaelib, even when, as a toddler, he tested my patience. I was warned about the terrible twos, but there was no mention of the "testing threes" or of the constant need for independence that, if not allowed, would be followed by fit-throwing. His shoes were not to have dew on them and by no means was I allowed to help when adjusting the Velcro that secured them to his feet.

Kaelib and I were living alone for the first time. I rented various apartments. I followed a pattern that when the lease ended, we would trade in for cheaper rent or a more favorable location. I could not be expected to stay put, as I'd never learned the importance of that concept. Jobs and houses came and went, as did the people who grazed my life, only to take up residence in my heart. It didn't matter— the homes or people—because I had Kaelib and he was the center of my world.

Most days were ordinary. After work I'd retrieve Kaelib from daycare and return home. With a quick check of the mail, we'd head to the park to play. Life was simple then, and aside from marveling at Kaelib's milestones and emerging personality, it teetered on boring. He kept me entertained with his make-believe stories and liked telling me about his new friends at day care. We often visited my parents and Zach, who lived just a few minutes away.

One day, I returned from work and, as always, made my way to the black mailbox at the end of the driveway of the small brick duplex. The dread of the envelopes that contained the demands, which I always fell short of paying on time, filled the box. As I thumbed through the mail, I was surprised to see a letter addressed to me with my former last name.

I flipped the TV station to *Bob the Builder*. With Kaelib happily entertained, I ripped open the envelope to reveal its contents. Inside was a letter that had been forwarded to me through the Social Security office. A letter from my father. It told a story that he had returned to Wisconsin, the last place we were rumored to have lived. He shared that during one stint in jail he'd been re-diagnosed from schizophrenic to bipolar. His concern was that I too contained the string of DNA, and unbeknownst to myself and my siblings, it coursed through our veins. He said that he wanted to rebuild the bridge that he'd burned when I was a girl, although no apology was written. He noted a number for himself and his case worker, if I chose to call him any time soon.

I contemplated the letter and consulted my mom for her opinion. Through the years she confided in me about the torture she'd endured during their marriage. She also reminisced on his good side and his sense of humor. He was a talented musician, and I even recalled hearing him sing. Sadly, his sudden outbursts of rage and violence overshadowed the good she'd seen in him. She explained that he believed the stories he told himself. If he thought the sky was purple, then he believed it to be true, regardless of the facts presented that proved it was indeed blue.

As it turned out, the many moves were due to his inability to hold on to a job. He would get fired for outbursts or because of his unorthodox behavior. In Texas, he came home one day with a car full of boxes and ordered us to pack. He blew through months of rent money on alcohol and women and had just been let go from yet another job. We drove off in the dead of night and days later arrived in Colorado.

My mother agreed that a conversation with him might bring closure. However, if I chose to take the risk and call him, it would need to be my decision and mine alone. I took great precautions and purchased a prepaid phone card with more than enough minutes to catch up on the fifteen years of estrangement. I drove to a nearby pay phone that couldn't be traced with a simple *69 and dialed the number of my father's counselor. I grilled her with questions, from his mindset to his temper. I questioned his medical history and his criminal history. I confirmed with her that the details in his letter were true, and then promptly dialed his number.

"Hello?"

"Hi, is this Larry?" I asked, not recognizing his voice.

"Yeah, who's this?"

My heart was nearly beating out of my throat as my hands shook, but I firmly held the black receiver that connected me to the man I spent a lifetime trying to forget.

"This is Harmonie. I got your letter," I stated.

"Hi, Harmonie! How are you?"

"I'm good. Actually, I'm great! You said in your letter that you have bipolar disorder, and that's why you wrote me?"

"Yes. I'm sure you remember some of the things that happened when you were a little girl, and it was all because I have bipolar. I wanted to let you know that you have a fifty percent chance of having it too," he explained.

"Well, I don't have anything wrong with me. I'm fine actually, no thanks to you," I sneered.

"I'm so glad to hear that. I'm glad you called. I sent letters to your brothers and sister too, but I haven't heard from anyone except for Bryan. Did you know he was in prison?" he asked without addressing the punch I threw in his direction.

"I did know, but I'm not telling you anything about them or where they are. You don't get to know that! I want to know how you could allow us to almost starve. Why didn't you help us?" I exclaimed.

"It wasn't easy for me either. If it hadn't been for some acquaintances of mine, I would have ended up living in a dumpster," he stated flatly.

"Yeah? Well, you weren't eight! What about mom? You used to beat her. You stalked us everywhere we went! Do you know how many times I had to move?" I questioned with every word reflecting a lifetime of anger.

"I remember Pam. She was a nice lady," he said with a voice devoid of inflection.

"She was a nice lady?! You were married to her for twenty years! I don't know why you sent me that letter. You may have taught me to ride a bike, but you were never a dad to me! My dad took care of me. My dad taught me to drive and my dad would never hurt me! I'm a mom now, and you will never know your grandchild. You'll never even know his name!" I told him, hoping that my words held enough hurt that they would jump through the receiver and punch him in the gut. Then he could know just a tiny amount of the pain he had caused me.

"I'm an idiot," he responded.

The line went dead, and for a moment I stood there staring at the metal number buttons on the pad and considered calling him back. I'd waited a long time to have this day, when I could tell him all the things I felt. I was sure he deserved to hear them. But all he could say to the wounds he'd created was that he was an idiot? I smiled and decided it was a fitting response. Yes, you are an idiot. Yes indeed.

At the time, all I knew about bipolar was that it made your mood change quickly. It had been a revision to "manic depression." I didn't accept this as an explanation or an excuse to the abuse he had put my family through. He'd been obsessed with finding us and preventing us from living any type of normal life. He wasn't able to tell me what I wanted to hear. Although nothing could take away the pain I experienced, and in the end, he and I both knew that. It would be many years later that I would come to understand the truth about his illness.

April, Justin, and my new niece lived just down the street, so naturally I expected to grow closer to her. I rarely saw her, though. She'd drop the baby off at my door and then return at the end of her shift to retrieve her daughter. Justin confided in me that his new stepdad would often argue with his mom and have violent outbursts. Justin's ever-growing urge to protect his mother led him to take some questionable actions and my concern grew for him.

With April keeping her distance, it was difficult to know what to do or even what could be done.

Then one day, I knew I could no longer stand by and do nothing. Justin was just a little boy and could do little to protect his new sister, his mom, and himself. My hands were tied when it came to the baby and April, but I realized that there was something I could do where Justin was concerned.

I made a call to the last place I remember his father had worked. He wasn't there anymore, but as luck would have it, they knew him well and how to get in touch with him. I asked that they give him my message, which consisted of nothing more than stating that it was his son's aunt and the phone number where I could be reached.

Shortly afterward, he returned the call. He was relieved to hear that his son was well. As it turned out, he'd sent birthday and Christmas presents for Justin at their last known address, only to have them returned as undeliverable. I filled him in on my concern for Justin, and he, along with my mother, made up a lie.

When Justin's father turned up the following week for a visit, I knew I had done the right thing. April was unaware of my betrayal since my mom had explained that Justin's father had gotten in touch with her, and she innocently shared her grandson's location. Justin's dad would continue to be a large part of his life, and I've never regretted my decision or the secret, that until now has never been

revealed.

Meanwhile, I was newly engaged to a very sweet

man who I met through work. Most southern men

wanted almost the same thing: a family. I wrestled

with that expectation that gnawed at my

nonconformity. When we announced the

engagement, my parents were overjoyed, David

especially. He'd grown quite close with my fiancé

and already considered him part of the family. My

mother immediately picked a day to shop for a

wedding dress, and it was purchased less than a

month later. The band was chosen, and we compiled

a long list of songs that we wanted to be played at

the celebration that was just six months away. The

details and days flew by, and I felt as though I was

unable to catch my breath.

Then, right before the holiday season was set to begin, my mom called. I sat in the bedroom I shared with my fiancé as I listened to the information she revealed. She'd received a call from someone from my past, and despite my being engaged, she decided I had a right to know. It was John, my high school boyfriend! I immediately burst into tears. For many years I'd searched for any indication of him, but wasn't able to find him. Even though I'd fallen in love with others, I had never completely gotten over him. I still thought of him almost daily. I didn't know what to do. I'd made a commitment to this man that I would marry him, yet John was so close.

The next day I dialed John's number, and we spent hours talking and catching up. It wasn't that he'd just thought of me, but he still loved me too, all these years later. The following week he flew out to see me. My fiancé was confident that nothing would change between us; however, I wasn't quite sure. I'd

pined for this person in a way I had with no one else.

But I wasn't a teenager anymore, and I knew I wasn't

the same girl John had once known.

I waited outside the restaurant, nervously twirling

my hair as I shifted my weight back and forth from

hip to hip. When he stepped out of the car, my head

swirled, and I caught a hint of dizziness as my heart

raced inside my chest. He'd changed into a man, and

I was caught off guard that my memory of him no

longer matched the reality. But within minutes, it

was as though no time had passed. Again, our hearts

leapt into one another. When I asked why he found

me, he responded that he missed my presence in his

life. Nothing more needed to be said . By the end of

the day, we shared a kiss, and I knew what needed to

be done. I returned to the home I shared with my

fiancé and, as gently as I could, announced that I

couldn't go through with the wedding. It wouldn't be fair to him when my heart still belonged to John.

John and I immediately agreed to a long-distance relationship, and less than a month later, we were back in each other's arms. We felt like teenagers again, but my new life as a single mom unsettled him. More than the reminiscing about the years before, we talked about our future. He too admitted that he wanted a family, and the time between us revealed that we had in fact become very different people. Yet by the end of the week he returned home with a promise that we would be married in a year.

Whether John and I married or not, I knew I had to make plans for my dreams. Three years after arriving in the small country town, I felt trapped. I wanted Kaelib to see that all things were possible. So, I decided that if I must stay in Kentucky, I would re-enroll in college. I'd already spent a year at the local music school, voice training and working on my confidence with public performance. Genni's husband and I formed a band, but after flowing through a handful of drummers and an unreliable guitarist, we called it quits. I continued writing songs, and when money allowed, I created demos that I'd send out to various corporations. The music scene was limited in Kentucky, and because I was on my own with Kaelib, I knew that furthering my education was a practical backup plan. But my restlessness grew, and by Kaelib's fifth birthday, I quit school to follow my passion for music and my dreams in Nashville.

Home of the South

Our new townhouse was adjacent to a vast field, just miles from downtown Nashville. At night, Kaelib and I would watch the fireflies light up like tiny little flashlights. I'd snatch one out of the sky and open

my hand for Kaelib to examine before it floated back

into the meadow, in search of an evening snack. The

bugs danced around the trees, illuminating their

branches as though they were wrapped in Christmas

lights. Those nights my heart was happily still.

April had asked to join me in the city for a fresh

start, but days later she took off, leaving only a note

to say she had changed her mind. The big city was

overwhelming and far away from Genni, the only

true support I knew. So, I decided to join the nearest

church. It also provided an opportunity for Kaelib to

join their preschool. The teachers were wonderfully

kind and encouraged Kaelib's growth. His brilliance

was not only noted but appreciated. One day after

picking him up, he asked me a question from his

booster seat in the back of the car.

"Mom, what would you do if you were a boy and you liked a girl?"

"How old is the girl?" I asked with a smile he couldn't see.

"She's five too, and I don't know what to say to her. It makes my belly tickle," he stated in all seriousness. I did my best not to laugh at the joy I felt from the innocence of his first crush.

"I suppose if I were a boy and I liked a girl, I would start by asking her what her favorite cartoon was," I responded, without a hint of a smile in my voice.

I was careful not to have him shy away from divulging his secrets and inner workings. With a thanks for my idea, he hummed along. I spied him through the rearview mirror, singing to the radio, as he watched the country road wind by through the window. I think of that moment from time to time.

His happiness and easygoing demeanor wasn't lost on me. I'd see children in stores throwing fits and crying. I'd look down to find Kaelib quietly organizing the merchandise on the shelves, so that all the items were facing the correct direction or grouped together accordingly. What a gift to have such a happy child. He was my little pea to my pod, and I too was happy.

While it was nice to have a pool at the complex, it didn't quite provide the serenity of an open body of water. On my next day off from work, I gathered up Kaelib and drove off in search of the nearest lake.

GPS didn't exist yet and I was tasked with navigating the busy streets and highways on my own. After some time, we pulled up to a sandy beach with moms and dads and their teens and toddlers. We quickly made our way to the shore where we made castles in the sand and waded in the water and I taught him to swim. It was a hot day that

dripped out humidity like a wet rag and from the

beach to the car, we were drenched in sweat again.

We welcomed the blast of cold air through the vents

on the way home. On the drive, I prepared my plan

to accomplish my goals of becoming the singer and

songwriter I dreamed of as a child. I hadn't given

much thought to being a single parent with little

financial support or support of any kind for that

matter, prior to the move. Now I thought of how I

might make the extra cash and scrape the money up

for an evening babysitter. Before I had much

opportunity to collect the cash that would afford me

the opportunity to perform, I found myself in a

horrific car accident.

On the same street that followed the turn to the lake,

I was T-boned by another car. It had peeled out in

order to cut across the three lanes of traffic and

struck me without warning. My car was not quite totaled. The damage, though, would certainly need repaired. I'd been spared any whiplash, but the pain in my hip became apparent when I stepped out of the vehicle. I stood at the front of my car, leaning onto it a bit, in hopes to give my hip a reprieve from the pain that seared down my leg. I asked for an EMT, but the officer gave me a once-over and directed the driver of the other car to retrieve my spare tire. He begrudgingly slung it on and sent me on my way.

Afterward, I drove over to Kaelib's preschool, just in time for late pickup, and returned home. I had difficulty climbing the stairs that led up to my room. So, I counted out two ibuprofens and grabbed the heat pack I had stowed away. That night, I lay on the couch and winced with every movement. When morning came, I relented and drove myself to the local clinic. The x-ray confirmed that my hip was dislocated.

The man who was in charge of fixing my car cut me a deal and told me to pay the rest when my lawyer was able to retrieve the settlement. My car was returned to me in subpar condition, but make-do repairs were all I could afford. I had no money saved, and because I was spending more and more time off from work, getting treatment for my hip, there was none to be saved. Finally, I scraped up enough for a storage unit and paid two men a hundred dollars to move my possessions.

Just like that, it was over. There in the city, under a dark sky, Kaelib and I stood outside of the front door where I'd once turned the key that held such wonder and hope. I dreamed of coming to this place and writing songs with other talented lyricists and musicians. I dreamed of singing at the local dive bars or maybe as a backup singer for an up-

andcoming artist. I believed that, through example,

Kaelib would learn to pursue his own dreams one

day, despite the challenges that came along and even

those I had created for myself.

We looked out at the field with the tall grasses that

separated the complex from the country house,

nestled beside the winding road. I was reminded of

a quote by John Lennon or maybe it was the

Brazilian author Fernando Sabino, as there has

always been much debate of the accreditation to the

original owner. "In the end it will be okay and if it's

not okay, it's not the end." I knew it didn't feel okay,

and so maybe it wasn't over. For the last time we

stood at the faded front door and watched the glow

of the dancing fireflies that drifted away, much like

my dreams.

The House That Grew Roots

I returned to Kentucky, only to be surprised with news that my grandmother on my dad's side had passed away and I was to receive an inheritance! After leaving Nashville with little more than a dollar in my pocket, I couldn't believe that I would now be able to make my dreams come true. But I wouldn't return to "Music City." Instead, I chose to reserve the money and live on the cheap. I rented a small duplex near Genni, in a sleepy quiet town.

Although I abandoned my dreams of becoming a singer/songwriter, my love for music remained. I used the inheritance to open my own business and called it Music Matcher. Its premise was to match musicians with others who sought to be in a band. During my own time in a band, it dawned on me the need for such a service, but until now it was only a passing thought. I also began managing bands and singers alike. I worked hard while balancing being a mom.

It was a luxury to be home each day when Kaelib returned from kindergarten. He would shower me with drawings and was quite talented for his young age. His homework was much too easy for him and he excelled well beyond counting to ten and ABC's by the time he was two. So, when I asked his teacher to encourage his intelligence, her remedy was to sit him in front of a computer and wait for the day when she wouldn't be bothered with the special child. That day came soon after. With the remaining inheritance, I enrolled Kaelib in a small private school.

While he thrived, the business struggled. Soon, I was given the opportunity to manage a talented artist who had quite the following. At just thirteen, she already had several music executives interested in her. Most weekends she would fly from coast to coast putting on performances and was well on her way to becoming the next big thing in pop music. I worked all of my contacts and resources and had a tentative contract from one of the top recording companies in the country. I did the legwork for free since I was still new to the industry, and I wanted to assure her mother that I was fit to manage her daughter. On the day she was set to sign with me, she forfeited. There was nothing more that could be done and while music ultimately broke my heart, this was the final blow to my bank account. The lack of income paired with my butting health problems brought Music Matcher to a close.

Years before, I suffered through two laparoscopies to diagnose my ongoing pain. It was revealed that I had endometriosis. In a matter of four years, I had three more surgeries, with the last being a

laparotomy. A four and a half inch incision was

made at my bikini line in order to access the

endometriosis that covered my colon in black and

tangled my uterus and ovaries in a web. It attached

to my bladder and although the surgeon worked on

this, she wasn't quite able to remove it entirely. She

was baffled at the stage of my illness after such a

short time from my previous surgeries. In passing, I

mentioned that the pain had been ongoing since my

teens and she marveled at the fact that I ever

became pregnant at all! I sometimes think about her

statement, although she's bound to have forgotten

the remark.

Kaelib was to be my only pregnancy and my only

child that I would ever know. I was never saddened

by this fact since a pregnancy hadn't been in my

plans, nor would a future pregnancy be. I had the

perfect love, and so how could I ask for more? I

could not imagine loving another human, regardless

of them being my own child, more than I loved him. I

didn't want to love another child because Kaelib was

all I needed and his love for me filled my heart and

my home. Every night when I'd tuck him into bed, we

would compete for who loved whom more.

I'd say, "I love you more than life."

He'd respond with, "I love you more than anything in

the world!"

I'd come back with, "I love you more than all the

planets in the universe!"

He'd try to one up me with, "I love you more than

anything in the galaxy!"

We'd go back and forth until I'd say, "I love you more

than all the stars in the sky!"

He'd laugh and tell me goodnight as I flipped off the light switch and turned on one of his mixed CDs to lull him to sleep.

After my long recovery from the laparotomy, I returned to work and found myself in accounting. I enjoyed the challenge of making sense of the figures, and it seemed I especially had a talent for forensics. I liked to say that being an accountant was similar to being a detective, and later it would prove to be just as dangerous.

A CPA I'd been working with acknowledged my gift of numbers and began referring his clients to me. I wasn't able to work a full-time job and keep up with a part-time business, so I turned the job into a client and worked years accumulating companies in need of a bookkeeper. I'd drive through town to each location, whizzing through numbers and banging out quarterly tax returns. My business was a success until the economy crashed and we entered the Great Recession. With only a handful of small clients left, I conceded and closed my business.

In the house that grew roots, I ended the relationship with John. The calls had become fewer and fewer, and two years had passed. He'd often call in the middle of the night and I'd try to understand the words he slurred through the receiver. The connection we once felt for one another was fading as though it had only been as strong as melting ice in a glass on a hot summer day. The last call came through the night Genni and I had gone dancing. The rare night that we took a break from our responsibilities and children. Something at the bar seemed to pull on my drunken heart strings. Later as she and I sat in her car, I cried buckets of tears. I wondered why John contacted me at all, only to string me along, smashing my heart to bits.

Then his name appeared on the Caller ID, and he asked why I was crying. We agreed that we must go our separate ways. The closure didn't instantly heal my heart, but the finality closed the chapter that I'd left open for far too long. Some believe that a person has one true soul mate, while others believe that there are many. I believe that our souls are not definitive. They grow and change. I believe that the possibility exists, that our souls seek one another in a way that is deeper than our egos and apprehensions. They're brought together, if only for a moment in time, for no other reason than they know they belong.

Where that relationship ended, I reestablished one with Bryan. Still in Wisconsin serving a long prison sentence, for what no longer matters. Bryan and I would spend week after week writing long letters to one another. We crafted a new relationship where the past severed itself from our present and for the first time, I was able to know him as an adult. He'd tell me of his plans to travel to Belize and we talked of a road trip. We reveled in the love we had for one another and the newfound friendship. He would draw pictures of flowers on envelopes that I would know were from him, before I ever glanced at the return address. I learned he too, loved to write songs. I would draft one and then send it along to him to add a verse or a chorus.

When I saw him that summer, he asked me to sing. In the loud visiting room, filled with strangers and inmates, I started off in a whisper and then allowed my voice to soar. With him there was no judgment, and I was not afraid. He'd tell me later that I sang better than the original. It made me smile, and I know to him, it was true. There were no facades between us. I accepted him as he accepted me, our faults, and flaws. I was simply his sister, and he was nothing more and nothing less than my brother. Through the many letters we exchanged, I found the sibling relationship I'd always wanted.

Several months after the visit, the phone rang, and I heard the familiar prerecording that announced I had a call from a state inmate. I happily accepted it. Bryan was on the other line with news. He received confirmation of his suspicions that he'd confided in me during my visit. The doctors finally ran an MRI, and the diagnosis revealed an inoperable brain tumor, the cause of his seizures and ever-growing headaches. He was told he only had four weeks to live. I retched from the pain of the news.

My mom, David, and I made the long drive to Wisconsin just before Thanksgiving to say our goodbyes. Bryan explained that his case worker might be able to get him out with something called a compassionate release, so that he could spend his

last days surrounded by the warmth of his family.

The parole board was reviewing his case again, and

now it was a waiting game. Bryan did not have time

to wait. When I returned home, I searched for ways

to help him. I searched for treatments at the

Cleveland Clinic, only to deduce that his tumor was

indeed inoperable. Then I began writing letters,

letters to the parole board and a well-crafted letter

to the governor of Wisconsin. With the letters and

the help of his case worker, Bryan was released right

before his birthday on December 12.

Christmas that year was divine. Bryan tagged along

with Kaelib and me for our traditional Christmas

light drive. We sang Christmas songs as we did when

we were kids. That tradition had fallen by the

wayside long ago when my mom married David, but

even David joined in. Prior to opening our gift, we

were required to sing a Christmas song. No song was to be repeated and must be finished before the first bit of tape was removed. It made Christmas take forever by the time I was old enough to sing, but that year, everyone wished that this Christmas would never end.

I remember I bought Bryan a fishing pole that year. A hobby he and I both shared. He would never get to use it, but I have many times since. It's still shiny red with a worn black handle. It leans against the hard basement wall, where I'll find it waiting for me to return to it in the summer and cast out the line.

The holidays came and went, and yet Bryan stayed. Past the four weeks and four months. Oftentimes, I'd take Bryan to my small duplex home for a break from my mother and she one from him. He welcomed his new role as an uncle and played with Kaelib as if he were his own. We'd watch movies and stuff our faces with homemade lasagna that I'd make with sausage, at his request. Other times, we'd listen to music from tunes we'd grown up on and to a new performer whom we both liked, named Kelly Clarkson. We'd wright songs together and sing. Meanwhile, he lost vision in one eye, but he still spent time painting. Some were masterpieces and some showed his deteriorating health.

Things were not settled between my mother and Bryan, and because I was not there, I cannot say exactly what transpired. Whatever her reasons were, my mother called his parole officer and asked that Bryan be sent back to prison. I refused to participate at the hearing. After all the hard work I did in helping to secure his release, I could not bring myself to send a dying man back to the cold and isolation of a lonely cell. My mother told me that when Bryan was handcuffed just before being transported back to prison, he told her that he hated

her. That he hated us all! I wasn't sure where they

returned him to, and I did not try to find out. I took

my mother at her word and decided to cherish the

time I had with my brother rather than engulf

myself in the hurt of it all.

Home Ownership

After closing my bookkeeping business, I found a

new well-paying job working for a man who was

neither nice nor kind. In fact, he was awful! I

pressed on to do my job despite his harassment and

constant mood swings. He'd call in the morning

joyously and ask for a report. Then by afternoon, he

would scream and threaten to terminate me. He

especially enjoyed torturing the women whom he

employed. When I was hired, I was tasked with

redoing years' worth of bank reconciliations. It

appeared quite a few amounts had been overlooked

and unaccounted for. I welcomed the challenge, and

for the next eight months, I worked diligently at

finding the missing money.

Meanwhile, the hefty paycheck afforded me the

opportunity to save enough for a down payment on

my very own home. In the same small town as Genni

was a large new neighborhood with rounded streets

and rolling hills and on the corner sat a one story

three-bedroom ranch. I knew when I saw it for the

first time, that it would be mine. The builder even

allowed me to choose the warm oak cabinets that

glistened in the light from the French doors that

opened onto a large back deck with a sprawling

view of the yard.

The large master bedroom contained a spacious

walk-in closet and a full bath with double sinks and

an oversized tub. In Kaelib's room I hung curtains

from cartoon-covered material he'd chosen and that I carefully stitched by hand. The vaulted ceiling between the dining and living room made the house almost echo, and for the first time, I realized that I didn't have enough possessions to fill the space.

Kaelib and I worked at planting a garden. Lettuce, green beans, and carrots. Most of the crop died. I had no experience, and the unfertile soil that consisted of thick clay mud did nothing to nurture its growth. I worked the landscape with colorful flowers of purple lavender and white, red, and yellow pansies that brightened the cement path leading to the front door. I spent hours shoveling through the hard clumps of dirt to make holes for the new trees I'd chosen. I imagined the years ahead and how they would flourish with brilliant leaves in the fall and shade in the summer.

My four-door car presented a challenge as to how to get the assortment from the store to the house, but I came up with a clever solution. I loaded them into the car through the sunroof! Gently, I'd hold the middle of the tree and ever so slowly begin to inch the base toward the floor of the car. As I drove down the road I'd laugh at the reactions from onlookers, who stared at the atrocity of the tree tops swaying in the wind. The house became our home, and I treasured not just the flourishing flowers, but my small family that included the addition of two charismatic cats.

When the season turned and winter came again, we set up a large Christmas tree and decorated the outside of our home with colorful lights. Every Christmas, Kaelib and I would do a craft project and this year, it was homemade gingerbread cookies. For hours we rolled out dough and carefully pressed the shapes of Christmas trees and snowmen into the sticky dessert. After transferring the cookies from the oven, we'd wait for the cooldown as the house filled with the sweet smell. Then we messily decorated each cookie with sprinkles of red and green and I delicately wrote names on the candy cane cut outs that completed our masterpiece.

I loved to make Kaelib laugh, and I'd find myself in stitches at my pure silliness. I didn't mind unleashing my inner child. I entertained him with ridiculous dances to various Christmas CDs. I'd bop and spin over to him with a serious face and grab him by the hands. Then we'd happily dance around the kitchen, pretending to waltz and twirl. We hilariously sang along to the holiday classics in funny voices that resulted in endless belly laughs. We were high on the sugar of the cookies and filled with Christmas cheer.

We continued that tradition for years. Eventually, he grew too tall for me to twirl and so I'd make him hold up his arm as I twisted myself under and back. I still make the cookies, albeit alone, and think of that first time. Our eyes filled with tears from the uncontrollable laughter and our hearts full of joy. Back to the days when we couldn't imagine a life without one another.

The toxicity of my employer became even more unstable by the time the new year arrived. When the alarm went off each morning, my heart would race so hard my whole body would shake. I began to suffer from migraines and the only reprieve were Saturdays with my son. Sundays were a day long mental preparation for Monday, where the twisted cycle started all over again. I tried to be grateful for the paycheck that provided me with financial security I hadn't known before, but the cost to my overall health was beginning to take its toll. So,

when I was fired a week into the new year, I was

happily relieved!

With just a small unemployment check, I knew it

wouldn't be enough to make my car payment, which

was just shy of being paid off, let alone the mortgage

payment. It wasn't long afterward that I received a

call from an attorney. I, as well as the other

employees, were under an official investigation for

embezzlement. I was in utter shock. I didn't even

know how to spell *embezzlement*, let alone have the

wherewithal to commit it! My former boss cooked

up a scenario in which the missing money I'd been

hired to find was stolen by none other than me!

To make matters worse, I was diagnosed with

earlystage cervical cancer, just in time for my

thirtieth birthday! The endless hormones I'd

consumed to control the endometriosis had likely

been the culprit. Regardless of the reason, I was uninsured and was faced with medical treatments that I couldn't afford. The stress overwhelmed me. I'd wake in the mornings with my heart in a rapid surge of anxiety and trudge out in search of a new job. Because the recession was still in full swing, I and the hundreds of applicants that applied for the same job waited for a call that never came. My stomach churned when the time came to look inside the full box that was stuffed with letters from attorneys and doctors. The remaining money I had saved to purchase the house quickly dwindled away, along with what now seemed like nothing more than a fantasy of home ownership.

Then one night, Kaelib woke to tell me of a bad dream where he could hear a strange noise that alarmed him. He climbed in bed beside me for comfort, but I was suddenly struck with severe stomach pains that hadn't jolted me from my slumber, but that I only felt when Kaelib came into the room. I ran to the bathroom and fell to my knees with the pain growing worse. In tears I heaved over, lying face down in a ball. Then just as quickly as it came, it passed. The next morning I woke to find my car gone. The strange sound that Kaelib had woken to, was none other than the repo truck.

I did everything I could to save my house. I sold the refrigerator and the stove. The once beautiful kitchen sat stark and barren. Finally, there was nothing else to sell and I abandoned what I had hoped would be my forever home. I bounced between my parents' house and Genni's. My only reprieve was a new activity that I quickly fell in love with due to its ability to quiet my mind and think of nothing aside from my breath and the pose that I held.

A couple times a week Genni would join me at the local gym, where a yoga class was only five dollars. I'd breathe in, hands flowing toward the blue mat that my bare feet grounded to. Breathe out, I'd stretch my legs behind and allow my neck to dangle in a pose called downward dog. I needed that hour to stop my heart and head from going too fast. A moment where I was at peace in my mind and when I did not think of the outcome of the investigation and pending lawsuit.

I'd breathe in, closing my eyes and stretching into warrior three. I didn't think of the rides I asked for to get me to my new place of employment or how long it would take to save enough for the transportation I was in such desperate need of. Breathe out, I did not think of the treatment I endured to remove the cancerous cells or the bills that followed that I knew I couldn't pay. The quiet would come to rest inside me until child's pose,

where I'd lie motionless, and my racing thoughts

would return.

I finally was able to afford a run-down duplex in one

of the only bad areas in the small town. We

unpacked only the necessities. It was a far cry from

my beautiful home. It lacked bountiful windows and

walk-in closets. There were no bathrooms with

double sinks or a spacious kitchen. There wasn't

even a dishwasher! There was one bathroom with

one sink that would have fit inside my old walk-in

closet two times over, with room to spare. The

duplex was brown on the inside and dingy and

matched my life as it was in the moment . . . dark.

Just after settling in, I received a call from the

Wisconsin prison. Bryan had died. Four years had

passed since his initial diagnosis, but the time

between did not prevent me from the sorrow that

crawled inside me and brought with it endless tears.

I cried for so long and so hard my shoulder locked

up from hunching over in grief. I could no longer

turn my neck, as it hung down for hours reading the

letters I'd received so long ago. A large package

arrived days later that contained the contents of his

life over the last several years.

Social media has given the better part of the world a

chance to reconnect with lost loves and old school

friends, and I used the opportunity to reach out to

Dan. He had a right to know that his brother had

died, and I felt it was my duty as Bryan's executor to

call him. I had never looked Dan up or spent much

time thinking of the person I no longer knew. It was

far better that he exist only in my memory, where I

could cherry-pick the moments that made me smile,

although few such moments remained.

Hours after sending a short message to his inbox, my phone rang with him on the other end. I hadn't considered how the conversation might go or imagined what his voice might sound like, as I'd long forgotten it. He could have approached me from behind, calling my name, and I wouldn't have recognized it. It seemed a lifetime had passed. Besides, he was more than a full-grown man now.

I had no other motivation than to share the news, but I found myself in a long conversation. He was gentle and careful with his words, and it was obvious he didn't want to upset me and have me end the call abruptly. Just a few minutes after we started talking, he unexpectedly made me laugh, despite the overt sadness and the reason that brought us together. I welcomed the reprieve from the grief during our conversation. I didn't bring up the past and was careful to protect my location since he admitted that he had created a new relationship

with our father. But I was taken aback when Dan

revealed he knew where I was.

Dan had been in contact with Bryan over the last

couple years, and just a year earlier Bryan had given

Dan a letter to mail to me. The letters Bryan had

sent had gone unanswered, and he assumed I did

not want to talk to him. He believed Dan would mail

the letters, and that I would open them. In truth, I'd

found no reason to forward my mail, since I didn't

presume that he'd want to contact me. The last I'd

heard, Bryan had been returned to prison with hate

in his heart for not just my mother, but for me as

well. The fact was, Bryan confided in Dan that he

indeed did love me and had missed me in the years

leading up to his death. My tears again found their

way to the edge of my eyes and streamed in silence,

as my heart slowly tore apart with the realization

that I missed those last precious years unnecessarily.

Dan found comfort knowing that his brother was no longer suffering and regretted that he too had let years slip away between them when he was a younger man. He also found humor in his impulsiveness in his youth and admitted that he still struggled with drugs, which propelled him into jail, time and time again. By the time the call was winding down, he apologized for his many cruelties and inappropriate behavior he inflicted on me as a child.

I heard the sincerity in his voice, and I knew that he had no other motivation than to extend his regret for the wrongs he'd done. We spoke several times afterward. Once on my birthday, he called and sang the familiar tune. Then he laughed a laugh that was reminiscent of the days before, when we were all children with so many reasons to cry but chose to

smile instead. Then, just as quickly as he had

reappeared in my life, he was gone again.

On a frigid winter's day, just before Thanksgiving,

David drove Kaelib and me to northern Indiana,

where we spent the day of thanks with my aunt.

Then the three of us made the journey up through

Wisconsin the day after the holiday. April arrived

separately with her children in tow. She and I didn't

speak, nor did we console one another. We were not

there to reconcile our estrangement, only to extend

our goodbyes to the brother we both lost much too

soon and yet so long ago.

The ground was hard and cold. The temperature

stood at twenty-two degrees, and the grass was

white with frost, despite the bright sun shining

down. The wind whipped my face and ripped

through my hair but did little to dry the continuous

stream of tears that seemed to be in freefall from my eyes. There we stood, the few who gathered in the small potter's field, outlined by a short, black cast iron fence and the barren trees that had shed their leaves months before. The men who unloaded the casket faltered as they were trying to lower it into the ground, momentarily revealing Bryan's exposed toe and part of his foot. I cried at the sight and the irrational thought of how he would forever be cold without the dressing he so rightfully deserved. I pulled out my phone and hit Play. The trumpets drifted out of the speaker as it sang the melody that would lull him to eternal sleep.

Beautiful dreamer, wake unto me,

Starlight and dewdrops are waiting for thee;

Sounds of the rude world, heard in the day,

Lull'd by the moonlight have all passed away!

Beautiful dreamer, king of my song,

List while I woo thee with soft melody;

Gone are the cares of life's busy throng,

Beautiful dreamer, awake unto me!

Beautiful dreamer, out on the sea

Mermaids are chanting the wild lorelie;

Over the streamlet vapors are borne,

Waiting to fade at the bright coming morn.

Beautiful dreamer, beam on my heart,

E'en as the morn on the streamlet and sea;

Then will all clouds of sorrow depart, Beautiful dreamer, awake unto me!

That spring, the investigation and lawsuit came to a close. In the end, my former bosses' right-hand man

was convicted of the embezzlement. The lawsuit

against me was dismissed with prejudice. I

remember getting the call from my attorney and the

letter that followed, absolving me of any liability. It

took many years to work past the abuse of my

former boss and the destruction of my life. But I was

determined to do something meaningful. At the time

I had no idea what that was, only that I would put

one foot in front of the other and create something

new.

In celebration, Genni and I planned a trip together.

Since having her daughter, Genni had only gone on a

couple of mini adventures with me. One trip was to

Nashville, where we danced and sang the night away

at a concert by one of our favorite bands. With our

children growing older, we planned a longer journey,

back to Mackinac Island. It had been almost fifteen

years since we stepped foot on the island that had

brought us together, and we were thrilled to relive a moment from our youth!

We'd returned only once before. It was Fourth of July weekend, and I found myself a bit homesick. We borrowed Genni's mom's old Toyota pickup, since the Caprice was in no condition to make the journey. We departed straight from work, and just after leaving the edge of town, Genni admitted she was too tired to drive. I happily jumped in the driver's seat and shifted my way along the highways and backroads of Wisconsin to the Upper Peninsula.

Genni slept soundly as the miles and hours passed by. I reclined the seat for comfort as the night darkened the road before me. Genni awoke suddenly. Startled, she yelled for me to wake up! In unison, I had looked down at the speedometer at the same moment she had opened her eyes, making it appear as though I too was sleeping. I burst out with a roaring laugh as I mocked her shock. She crossed her arms and sat back in the seat, unamused.

Morning broke over the horizon and the waves that ran parallel to the two-lane road splashed along in sync with the bump of the pickup's tires. It wasn't long after that we arrived at the ferry. The boat filled with visitors, and it occurred to me that we were now fudgies, a term used by locals to describe tourists. We amused ourselves with the epiphany as much as we shunned the idea. After departing, we began making our way to the quaint B&B we had rented when, all of a sudden, a cute boy on a bike approached us. It was my ex-boyfriend from the season before.

He had the same smile, and I lit up at the sight of him, despite myself. We spent that first night together talking until morning. When the sun rose, it brought with it not just a new day but forgiveness.

My heart had healed from his indiscretion and the pain of the betrayal. Although I would never be able to face the man from the year before, that night at the top of the hill, the one I could neither forget nor remember, on some level I made peace with it or at least found a way to live with it.

Closure is a remarkable thing. It can calm our anger and bring us tranquility to tame our tortured souls and mend our broken hearts, all at the same time. Not all moments promise it, but in the light of that Fourth of July day, I held it in my hand. I felt the solid weight of the gift wholeheartedly given to me, and I was finally able to leave the past behind me.

This trip would be different, as wiser adults with time and space between the past. In the early morning light, we climbed into the car and kissed our children goodbye and headed down the twisting roads of the blue grass to the interstate. We reminisced as we made our way through the

flatlands of Ohio and the familiar hills of Michigan.

Each song on our road trip playlist was blasted

through the speakers as we both sang out of tune at

the top of our lungs. Our excitement grew when we

boarded the ferry.

Upon first sight, nothing had changed. From the

dock, I saw the same houses that stood in a row,

frozen in time. The horse carriages trotted past as

though they were on a reel with a constant loop. We

passed by the shops where we once had developed

our own sign language that would compel the other

to ask for a break or lunch hour. Now we were

replaced with young girls, much like we once had

been.

The farther we hauled our luggage down the street,

the more unfamiliar the island became. The once

prized coffee shop had been turned into a

laundromat and the corner store was now a

Starbucks. The bar with the couches where we spent

many a night, listening to the songs of a one-man

acoustics band, was remodeled into a run-of-themill

sports bar. But the lake and the park stood

unchanged, as though it had waited for our return.

There were some welcome changes to the island as

well, which also included a new activity we were

excited to try. We met with the instructor the next

morning. After securing our life vests and listening

to the directions, we carefully climbed into the small

orange vessels and practiced our paddle techniques.

The late May day was bright with sunshine, and we

giggled as we flung water at one another. Our

instructor clicked the camera to capture our

adventure and the beauty that could only be seen by

boat. We stalled for a moment to gaze down through

the clear water and observe the large catfish and

bass that swam alongside and under our watercraft.

As we sat atop the gentle waves, I reflected on the years before.

The island had unwittingly changed me. As most youth eventually do, I sought to find myself here and to become more me than I had known before. My trajectory had been changed when I arrived here, in what now felt as though another lifetime ago. If I hadn't gone to this place, I wouldn't have met Genni or become pregnant with Kaelib. Maybe it always was destined to be, if I were silly enough to believe in such a thing. Maybe our souls would have always found their way to one another. There was no way to know for sure, only that in this present, it existed.

The wind had shifted and the ease of the paddle on the way out hadn't prepared me for the two-knot waves that demanded I use all my strength. I dug into the water as the kayak lifted up and then down between the crests of the waves. My breath revved up as I heaved the paddle into the cool water, switching quickly from left to right as I fought to steer my boat to shore. When we finally returned to land, our arms were weak with exhaustion and our legs quivered from the tension of balancing the boat. We decided that the only logical thing was to return to the B&B for a shower and spend the evening doing the infamous bar crawl!

We donned our T-shirts that required a signature from each location as proof that we participated in a drink, with bragging rights as the only prize for finishing. At the first bar we collected one signature and their coaster as a keepsake. One after another, bar after bar, we ordered shots and beers. Shirts were signed, often with good-luck wishes and funny phrases. By the end of the night, we found ourselves at the pier where Genni and I had spent many evenings talking and singing and enjoying the

friendship that few others could know or

understand.

The stars sparkled upon the lake as the click of the

small waves brushed against the beams of the mossy

pier beneath us. Our legs dangled over the water as

we sat, inebriated, with glassy eyes and rosy cheeks.

We marveled at our friendship and all it had

endured. We talked of the past and pondered the

future and our dreams of what was to come. I

confided in her my loss of direction. The struggles of

the last few years had transformed me, and I knew

that I was no longer the same woman. I'd known

many failures, like the music company and my

diminished dreams of becoming a singer. I didn't

believe in destiny and yet also believed I was

destined for something more. I could not say with

clarity what that was but confessed an idea I'd

secretly been toying with in my imagination.

Home Is Where the Heart Is

For obvious reasons, I hadn't enjoyed much of my life in Kentucky. I felt as though I was water, and it was oil. In some respects, it was similar to when I'd moved to Wisconsin as a girl, only in reverse. My lack of a southern accent was noted, and the small town provided little to do. Not even a body of water was close by, yet I stayed. Kaelib deserved the stability that I had never known. I chose to sacrifice, if seeing him thrive and fulfill his dreams was a sacrifice at all.

To make up for my disdain that I associated with my experiences in that state and when money allowed, I traveled. My vehicle represented my freedom and I'd find myself taking off on a whim to Tennessee for long weekends. Kaelib and I would adventure through the woods and explore the little tourist towns. I loved making new mom and son memories and watching his curiosity unfold in the museums we frequented or experiencing his wonderment at the sight of snow-covered mountains.

Two times before, we made the trip out to California. From the highway along the coast, I'd veer off to the side of the road and we'd stand in awe of the blue ocean that beckoned us to explore it. We watched the dolphins romp in the sea and the surfers who splashed by on their boards. No sooner did we climb back into the car than I'd pull off again to view the vast and ever-changing beauty that surrounded us.

I remember sitting on the sandy beach in Carlsbad. The tide had started to rise and although we were fully dressed, we rolled up the bottoms of our pants and pushed up our sleeves and ran to the edge of the shore. Holding each other's hand, we'd jump wave after wave. I still remember Kaelib's laugh. We took turns with the camera, capturing the moment just before our clothes were drenched with salty water from the sandy surf. The flash of the camera cemented the happy moments that would remind us of the times we shared in the bright blue water.

Every summer we took an annual trip to a little town called Santa Claus, where we spent our time at the theme park. When the tradition started, Kaelib was just old enough for the little train rides and swings. As time wore on and he became older, we moved to the water rides and the wave pool. I loved arriving at the park early, before the droves of people and lines of eager children. We would climb the stairs of the first water slide and go splashing down into the cool pool beneath it, only to climb the stairs and splash down again. As always, we'd stay until the park closed.

On Friday nights, the theme park would put on a vast display of fireworks. I remember watching them as we sat in the night air alongside the Koi pond adjacent to the holiday-themed hotel in the center of town. Each bang and boom blasted with an array of colors from red to purple to orange and green. When the show ended, we'd return to our little green tent that sheltered us from the raccoons finding us in our slumber. That was our place. It was our getaway from the staleness of the little town in which we lived and the monotony of day-to-day life. I welcomed the interruption from the mundane, but it was the precious time with my little boy, who was too quickly growing into a man, that I treasured.

Meanwhile, April returned to Kentucky again. Like me, she'd never known a home, only a brief feeling of belonging. Year after year, she'd move away, then return with a growing group of children and ask my mother and David for assistance. My parents' large home sat on the side of a hill, overlooking a long grass valley surrounded by pines and oaks and shrubs with colorful wild berries.

My mother had called the house her retirement plan. She'd worked on the blueprints for years. It wasn't unusual to find her at the kitchen table late at night with a scrap piece of paper and a sketch of a house. But this was the one that she drew and knew immediately that she had to build it. She even built the home to scale from Legos as a demonstration. She meticulously created the designs, along with the square footage of every room and closet. It was no surprise, since she was a phenomenal mathematician!

When I was a little girl, I would test her abilities with a calculator game. I'd make up outlandish calculations, and we would race to see who could come up with the answer the fastest. I'd push the

numbers into the calculator as quickly as my fingers

could go, but before I could get through even half of

the equation, she would confidently state the

answer. I'd look up to see her nonchalantly sitting

there, with her notorious eyebrow raised, as if she

were waiting for me to check her math.

When the house was completed, she again made her

mark in every room, with curtains and paintings

and rugs that finished out the decor. Greenery and

cactus plants with pink and orange flowers were

placed along the windows in the oversized sunroom

that looked out onto the wraparound deck. I

remember her gushing while giving me the grand

tour when I visited for the first time. I was so proud

of her accomplishment and the woman I'd grown to

know—as not just my mother, but my friend.

It was more than enough room for my parents and Zach but was not constructed to hold April and her children. I did my best to mend the breach between us, despite my deepening resentment. I was only too happy to form new relationships with my nieces. I admired the three girls for their resilience between the many moves, I understood all too well. They reminded me of my own sister and me, in the times in the trailer and the closeness I once knew with her, so many years ago. Justin had just joined the military, and once a week I'd send letters filled with adult jokes that I knew would make him laugh and encouraging words that I hoped would give him strength. He'd write back when the exhaustion of boot camp would ease and tell me of the goings-on as best he could, always thanking me for thinking of him.

April's need for help never ceased, and I never asked for much because she'd taken more than what was her share and left little for me. So, when my parents lent me three thousand dollars, I thanked them for their generosity. I bought an old car to replace the one that had been repossessed. With the remainder, I enrolled in school where I trained every weekend for the next six months to receive my accreditation as a yoga therapist. The secret I shared with Genni, that night on the dock.

I learned the different varieties and styles of yoga, as well as the many asanas. I was especially fond of the meditation techniques, coupled with the study of Dharma. Unlike karma, where whatever you put out comes back to you, dharma is a more complex theory. Like peanut butter to jelly—smooth, that's dharma. Oil and water are just the opposite. Dharma is not just about the individual, but all people.

I often remind myself about dharma when I'm stuck in traffic. I tap the steering wheel and strain my neck to peer over to the right side of the car from the driver's seat. My mind starts with the usual annoyance and rhetorical questions. *What's going on? Why are we stopped?!* Before I let my anger run away with me, I remember that my dharma is to be here. Maybe because I'm here, I've avoided some disaster down the road. Then I see an angry driver who is weaving in and out of traffic and illegally down the shoulder, obviously in a hurry to get somewhere. It doesn't concern me. I do not know the load he carries, and I try to imagine what has fueled his behavior. The calm of Dharma reminds me that I am not an island and that I'm right where I'm supposed to be. I will be here until I'm no longer meant to be and then, I will be someplace else.

After receiving my accreditation, I began teaching full time. I'd start the class by reminding my students to let go of their expectations. Might today be the day that your body moves into a pose that it had refused the time before? I had been inspired myself by the small phrase that held such a magnificent idea. Expectations. The ultimate choice we make to believe the outcome will go as we imagine. The compliment we believe we deserve; the reward we work hard for and believe we have earned. Expectations. We hold on to them as though it will be indefinite because we believe it to be, but life does not always live up to them. People especially, disappoint in ways that could not be fathomed. Yet, we may expect a ticket for speeding, only to be given a warning. We may expect to not be forgiven for a mistake, yet instead find a hug and acceptance. I loved my work and the guided meditations that I incorporated at the end of each practice. They not only calmed my students but gave me a reprieve from my tired muscles and achy joints, a result of the many hours of relentlessly moving my body. Just like muscles that must be torn in order to change and grow, I emerged anew.

A calm had taken up residence inside me. Dharma opened my heart in ways I was unprepared for. But how do you prepare for something you didn't know existed? I'd never been good at letting things go. Admittedly, I was a packrat and my emotions had been no different. I held them inside of me, not just as lessons, but as a shield. If I were to let them go, I would become unarmed and left vulnerable to new pain and old hurt. Yet now I was able to release them. The lawsuit and the anxiety, the fear of the past and of the unknown. I had healed, letting go of my own expectations, and I opened my heart to new possibilities.

One evening Genni sat beside me as I lay on the table at the local tattoo shop. When the buzzing ended, I looked down at the purple Sanskrit letters that read: Dharma. My reminder to follow mine and to remember the wholeness and peace I was finally able to achieve. I'd admire the ink at times when my heart still raced too quickly, and I'd use the meditative routine to steady the thumping that pounded in my chest.

With the Great Recession still in full swing I struggled to keep the studio open and earn enough to pay my bills. I again was faced with closing yet another business, but I had to provide for Kaelib. Without another alternative, I agreed to a lowpaying position doing sales at the only job I could find. A week later I arrived in Ohio for a work conference, and forty-eight hours later, I knew I had finally found home!

I returned to Kentucky and parted ways with my employer. With Kaelib on board and just as excited for a fresh start, we collected our boxes that we had never fully unpacked. I fetched Zach, who decided that he needed a new opportunity as well. I was thrilled to leave Kentucky! I was thrilled to leave the past behind and intrigued by what the future would bring. Zach, Kaelib, and I talked of all the possibilities as we drove along the highway. I became as giddy as a child on Christmas morning as we passed under the sign that read: WELCOME TO OHIO.

House of Lies

To me, living in an apartment wasn't ideal, but the spacious three-bedroom was inviting with its electric fireplace and sunken living room. We were nestled between the top and bottom floor. Because it happened to be an unusually warm winter, Zach, Kaelib and I often gathered on the balcony to chat and watch the traffic pass by, and did our best to ignore the smell of curry wafting up from the apartment below. The fact was, it was perfect, at least for now and I was content to be far away from the past, that loomed just south of the border.

I took the first job I found but the position was a bit remedial. I didn't mind that much, and I viewed it only as a pit stop that would enable me the ability to pay the bills until I secured a position that was more befitting. I found it a bit odd to begin a new job on a

Thursday, but I welcomed the opportunity to make a bit of cash before the week rounded out. Friday was my birthday, and I was excited at the prospect of purchasing a new cell phone, as well as indulging in a lavish dinner in the city.

On Friday morning I jumped right into work. I answered phones and made copies, deliriously joyous to have a fresh start, even if the position was the furthest thing from my dream job. Late in the morning, a man appeared at my desk. I greeted him as I was instructed to do when visitors entered the building. He announced the company he was with and handed over a box of chocolate hearts for Valentine's Day. I smiled and told him that I'd require two boxes, one for Valentine's Day and one for my birthday. Without hesitation, he passed over a second box, along with his business card. With a quick thanks, he turned and left.

I eyed the candy and happily bit into one of the hearts that was filled with gooey caramel. Then, I looked down at the business card and was surprised to see a name I recognized. I emailed the address listed on his card and inquired about it. My grandparents shared his last name, and because it's unusual, we must be related, I wrote. Maybe we could meet one day for lunch and figure it out, I stated innocently, but eager to make a new friend. His response was that the relation came from his stepdad who bestowed the name to him.

Over time, we conversed about business matters, but the conversations quickly expanded to friendly chit-chat and bordered on flirtation. Although we were professional, he was easy to talk to and the conversations flowed. His intelligence shined through the receiver, and the exuberance he exuded was contagious. I was eager to craft a new life away from the stagnancy and anxiety of Kentucky. So, when he told me of his plans to play paintball, I asked if I could join.

I'd dated a variety of men, many of average height, with dark or blond hair. He was tall at six foot-two, with a pretty smile and bright blue eyes. When I descended the stairs the morning of the paintball outing to see him waiting in his gold truck, a bandana on his bald head and a slimming black shirt, there was not an overt attraction. It had been many years since I was in a relationship. Most were short-lived flirtations where I wasted my time until I grew bored and would happily entertain myself with singledom.

It became a running joke when I'd head out for a date. I'd tell Kaelib that I would bring back my leftovers, and he'd tell me to order something yummy and that he'd see me in two hours! We'd laugh because it was true. So, it hadn't occurred to me that this outing would be anything more than an opportunity to make friends with a man who seemed to have a zest for life and had already proved his ability to easily make me laugh.

For March, it was unseasonably warm. We drove with the windows down and listened to a playlist of songs he blared through the oversized speakers. An hour later, we arrived where his friends were waiting to break into teams. At the practice range he explained the rules. He stood next to me and watched as I pulled the trigger and completely missed the target at the end! I practiced a few more times, with him patiently coaching me. Finally, I saw the colorful splatter shoot out across the wooden board and we were ready to begin the first game. He was full of energy and eager to win. He also matched my love for competition. By the end of the game, my cheeks hurt from endlessly laughing and we were both exhausted from the many wins that crowned him "King of Paintball."

On the way home, we had time alone and I asked him about a rumor I'd heard the previous week.

"Are you married?" I asked without judgment.

He hesitated for a moment. "I am."

I arrived minutes later at the three-story complex and thanked him for the day. I headed toward my room for a quick shower and afterward, as I lay on the couch, replaying my first paintball experience on the warm Saint Patrick's Day, I texted him. "Thanks again for letting me tag along. It was really fun!"

"I'm glad you came along too. It was such a beautiful day! Almost as beautiful as you!" his response read. I closed my eyes and drifted off to dream of various scenarios, like a replay of that day that later seeped through my slumber as I laughed myself awake.

Kaelib was regularly out practicing his parkour skills. I thought nothing of his time away, since I urged the shy teenager to make friends. Every week I drove him to the city, where there was a small group who would practice for hours. Sometimes I'd stay and watch, while other times I'd return to collect him and listen to him retell the highlights and boast of his strength and sore muscles. He struggled with new friendships, and so by summer I allowed him to return to Kentucky and spend the time before school restarted with Genni. I'd call to check in, only to be told that he was out with one of his many friends that he'd accumulated in his former life.

This was the most time he and I had ever spent apart. Much of my life revolved around Kaelib and being his mother. From rides to friends' houses and endless activities, to planning trips and entertainment, and of course, the day to day of homework and school. But in the new city, I felt a world away without him. Although I'd made several new friends of my own, Kaelib would typically tag along on those outings as well. Now the apartment was empty. Zach worked many long days and nights and would return to his room, where he occupied himself with endless hours of video games and just as many beers, so I occupied myself in the arms of my married boyfriend.

I never thought of myself as someone capable of a forbidden relationship and one that clearly I had no business being a part of. Yet there was instantly an unspoken bond between us. Something that was so undeniable that being without him was like having the air sucked from my lungs: I'd hang in the balance before he'd return once more, and I could breathe yet again. He seemed to marvel at me in ways I'd never seen in myself. It was as if his soul had known mine all along. After only a few months, I resigned myself to the fact that I could no longer deny the feelings that had built up inside my heart. As we lay in bed in the dark and quiet of my room, I found the courage to whisper them.

"I love you, CJ," I said without expectation of a response. He kissed me deeply as he rolled me onto my back, and I let go of the notion that he might return my love.

But then he asked, "Do you love me, or are you *in love* with me?"

"Both," I answered.

With his lips pressed to my ear, in a hushed voice, he whispered, "Me too."

That summer we spent many nights in that room, talking of our shared experiences. He had lost his sister from cancer, who had also died near Thanksgiving, just a year after Bryan. We discovered that we had similar childhoods, where we both had not known roots, but agreed that Ohio had drawn us to a feeling of home. He was born in Idaho, but just moved back to California a year before I arrived at his birthplace, where my family and I stayed for a night at the little mountain campground on the lake. He was unlike the other men I had fallen in love with or had even known before. He challenged me as much as I did him. I loved our deep discussions about anything and everything. We talked of our dreams for the future and allowed our hearts to be honest, which may have been the only truth to the lie that we were living.

By the end of summer, he chose to be with me full time, only to change his mind days later. In his haste, he left his robe hanging on the back of my bathroom door, the only reminder of him that remained. Much like the cliché that I found myself living, I'd go into the bathroom, with swollen eyes that had run dry of tears, and put my arms through the oversize sleeves. The softness of the material would lay upon me as I'd smell the shower gel mixed with the lingering scent of his skin.

I'd lie on the empty bed wrapped in the warmth of the smooth cotton robe, imagining a day when his arms would be wrapped around me again. Unlike my previous relationships, where I'd depart due to the smallest slight, I begged him to stay. My pride no longer existed, along with my self-respect. I insisted that his love for me was real, but to no avail. He left and closed the door behind him. Distraught, I tried my best to swallow my new reality. It was a

forbidden love that I stupidly had invested my heart

into.

The remaining months in the apartment played out

like a soap opera, with CJ returning and then leaving

again. When the lease ended, I returned Zach to

Kentucky. During the hours of endless miles, I

warned him of his growing drinking and pleaded

with him to stop. I did my best to encourage him and

noted that the future would be better and that he

could return to the city when he saved enough

money to secure his own living quarters. Zach had

turned dark and depressed, and I took the twelve

years of wisdom I had on him to reassure him that

his life was worth pursuing. I knew this mindset too

well, and I'd also seen the other side of not giving

into my own pain. Life could be painful, but it didn't

mean it had to be permanent.

When we parted ways, Zach promised to try to heed my advice. I hugged the tall boy, who was now a fullgrown man and told him that he better, in my most stern older sister voice. I knew that Zach would find his way to wherever it was that he was to be. Time and time again, I created a new life and found new happiness in places I never knew to look. If I had given up, I may have never known the love of my son or the joy of a home I could call my own. It seemed that with every heartbreak, a new chapter began.

279

The House of Broken Hearts

I've never been much of a gambler, although I do leave a lot to chance. I moved to Ohio on a whim, not knowing if it was the right decision. I knew only that something inside me propelled my heart and head to work together, which doesn't happen as often as I'd like. I gambled on love, and I lost. What were the odds of finding love, or was I just lucky to have found it at all? It is entirely possible to die from a broken heart, but what are the odds of that?

After working nights as a waitress (the job I took after departing ways with the employer who forced me to have contact with the man I still loved) and early mornings spent teaching yoga for extra income, I realized I could not continue at that pace. I returned to the career that had once almost ended me. Accounting was familiar and easily paid the bills. Besides, I was really good at it, even if I didn't

enjoy it much anymore. So a month later I was all

too happy to knock down the many jobs I'd

accumulated to just that one.

The new townhouse was drab and dated but

affordable and presented the opportunity to enroll

Kaelib in one of the best school districts in the

country. Years ago, he and I decided against

accepting the prestigious invitation from Duke

University to join its TIP program. Now I encouraged

him to reconsider it for the upcoming school year.

There was a vast array of offerings at his new school,

and he carefully chose his classes.

He assured me that he was up for the challenge, and

I was confident in his abilities. Recently he'd shared

his sketch pad with me, and in between the doodles,

he configured his own algebraic equations. He never

ceased to amaze me, but his brilliance was always

outshined by his warm nature and sweet personality.

It was tradition to take a first day of school photo, and with Kaelib starting high school, I requested that he write his goal at graduation in large print on a poster board. Kaelib stood at the front door of the brick building; his wavy chestnut hair nearly hung down to his shoulders. I allowed him to grow it long without protest knowing it was just a phase. His wide smile held little indication of the person he was yet to become. His young innocence paired with his hazel eyes, illuminated his hopes and wonderment. I too had dreams for him. More importantly, I wished for happiness in whatever life he chose to live and profession he chose to pursue. In colorful lettering, Kaelib held the sign that boasted "When I graduate, I am going to go to college to get a degree in Physics." That picture is embedded in my mind.

With the school year in full swing, Kaelib struggled with the new environment of silver spooned children and the demands from the school that he pick a career. By midyear, though, he'd found his footing and hit his stride. He made a few friends, which drew him away from his studies. I was actually pleased by this. Although I knew the young teen was inherently smart, I believed it was just as important that he had a social life as well.

I've always believed in balance, and I highly recommend mistakes. Kaelib was a perfectionist from an early age and often cried when he fumbled. He suffered with a stutter as a preschooler and into the early years of elementary school. I'd often imagined that his mouth wasn't able to keep up with his mind. I'd stop him midsentence and tell him to slow down, think about what he wanted to say and start again. He disliked being corrected and would cry, yet over time my method worked. I sought to comfort him through logic and remind him that as humans, mistakes are part of life and one of the best ways we learn, as long as we're mindful and try not to repeat them. Teens especially will make many mistakes and even as a small child he learned that choices, good and bad, have consequences.

By the time my birthday rolled around the following year, I decided to head to Cleveland for an overnight stay accompanied by CJ, who finally made the decision to leave his marriage once and for all. His broken heart had longed for mine, and I felt that together we could conquer the world. I was overjoyed to take a trip with the man I had so deeply fallen in love with, yet I found myself anxious at the thought of Kaelib staying behind.

It was the first time I'd ever left Kaelib alone overnight, but at fourteen he was a responsible young man. Certainly, he could manage a night without his mother. Unlike my childhood or my generation for that matter, where children were left alone more often than not, I didn't want Kaelib to experience that loneliness. But there came a time to also learn responsibility. So, I programmed my friend's number from work into his phone and reassured him, as well as myself, that in an emergency she would be there in less than ten minutes. I was sure to tell him to be by his phone, since checking in every three hours was essential to me being able to enjoy the other 178 minutes until the next call.

CJ and I explored the city and museums and shivered in the cold of the woods as we set out on the path to see the waterfall that had iced in the frigid temperatures. CJ climbed the frozen banister

and carved our initials into a tree that still stands

today. Because of the Valentine's Day rush, the

restaurants were packed, and we turned away

numerous times due to the long waits. Not only was

it necessary to celebrate my birthday with an

appropriate meal, we were also famished from our

day of exploration.

Finally, I called a much too fancy establishment who

happily stated they did not have a wait and would

see us shortly. Donning our worn jeans and our tees

that boasted "Rock and Roll Hall of Fame," we pulled

up to the valet and dropped the keys off to the older

model Corolla with the driver. We were, in fact,

seated immediately; however, our apparel stood out

amongst the sea of dates, who without a doubt had

spent much of their evening meticulously preparing

themselves for an extravagant night out. We both

ordered a mediocre steak and filled ourselves with laughter at our own audacity. The next day, I returned home to an unharmed Kaelib sitting in front of the TV with a bowl of mac-n-cheese. We had made it through our first night apart.

In the early days, my and CJ's relationship was more than rocky and could best be described as tumultuous. He was grappling with the upended emotions left over from ending his marriage, and we continued to have many makeups and breakups. Just weeks after returning from Cleveland, we parted ways again. As I sat on my yoga mat and focused on each breath to calm the rocketing heartbeat that I told myself was anxiety, I felt my mind begin to slow down.

By now I was well aware of the part I played in the drama that was my relationship. However, in the stillness I had an awakening (or ah-ha moment, if you will). I felt the depth of my irresponsible choices. I felt the pain (of which I was partly responsible for inflicting on the unintended victim) and her own anguish and heartbreak, which I hadn't given much thought to. There was nothing I could change. I could only admit to my part and own the actions that caused harm and heartbreak for everyone involved.

When I taught yoga, as a way to focus and ease anxiety, I would say, "Yesterday has passed, and tomorrow is not promised. Five minutes from now is not guaranteed. All we have is this moment." All I could do in the moment was own my truth. To own it requires raw honesty within yourself and the courage to acknowledge it. It's part of the yoga philosophy I vowed to honor when I began my education as a yoga therapist. The simple act wouldn't change the outcome but would allow me to feel wholeheartedly the impact of my decisions and the wisdom to not repeat the same mistakes. The truth was, I had played an integral part in breaking my own heart, and I alone would need to be the one to repair it.

The palpitations returned with a vengeance, and I found myself preparing for a heart ablation. Genni made the drive and joined me at the hospital. I reminded her of her official status as Kaelib's godmother should anything happen to me. Patiently I lay in my hospital gown awaiting the nurses who would whisk me away to where the doctor would identify and ablate the extra electrical pathway to my heart that I had no doubt been born with. Kaelib and Genni sat with me as I bravely reassured them that I would be fine. There was no reason to be concerned, I told them. The doctor had performed this procedure hundreds of times, and the recovery would be a breeze. Plus, I would no longer need to be concerned by the unexpected racing heart that had landed me in the hospital twice before. Those experiences were far more intense!

I remember the first time. I was sitting on CJ's couch, waiting for him to shower and dress for a Halloween festival we'd planned to attend. Just as I opened my second beer, the familiar pounding started. Unlike the many times before, it didn't slow with meditation or deep breathing. By the time CJ was midway down the stairs, my whole body was jerking uncontrollably. We arrived at the hospital minutes later, where they rushed me into a room. I lay there watching the heart monitor as it read out a rate upward of 220 beats per minute. Then the doctor injected me with a potion that stopped my heart completely. CJ held my hand as we anxiously saw the machine flatline. My eyes stared in wait, as well as the nurses nearby who had already prepared the paddles that would bring me back if my heart decided to remain quiet.

When the nurses were certain I was prepared, I hugged Genni and Kaelib and they wheeled me back to the cold operating room. Great precautions were used in sterilizing the room to ensure that germs could not travel through the entrance of my artery that led to my heart. I was transferred to the table and covered in warm blankets and then and only then, I cried. The nurse lovingly scolded me as I reached to wipe the tears from my cheeks. She tucked my arm back under the heated blanket and retrieved a tissue. She blotted my tears with her gloved hand, and I confessed that I was scared! Her upside-down face smiled at me as she reassured me that I'd be alright. Then the doctor appeared by my side, and they worked as a team to calm my fears.

Several times during the procedure, I awoke with

pain in my jaw, and I'd feel my heart pounding like

drums in my chest. I looked over at the doctor and

saw him sitting in front of a monitor with a team of

white coats surrounding him. I asked if he'd found

the cause yet because my jaw and shoulder hurt, but

before I could hear his answer, I was asleep again.

One time I opened my eyes and looked up at the

screen next to me. I could see the long tube that had

made its way from my groin to my heart. I hadn't

been scared then, but intrigued at the procedure

and the notion that I was looking at my heart being

operated on. I glanced at the doctor, who

concentrated on the preciseness of his talent, and

then he noticed my open eyes. "Give her more

juice!" he proclaimed to the nurse as I drifted back

into darkness.

By no means do I consider myself a good patient.

Blame it on my zodiac or my free spirit, although it's more likely that I don't enjoy the feeling of being helpless. So after five minutes in the recovery room, I was ready to leave! It felt like an eternity before I was released and returned home. Being cared for is also not my strong suit. It's not news to anyone that knows me, that I can be more than a bit stubborn. Thankfully, Genni was there to insist that I sit on the couch with my leg propped up and allow her to entertain me with card games and antidotes of her life in Kentucky. While Genni played nurse, Kaelib snuggled next to me and gently rested his cheek on my chest, listening to the beats that pounded rhythmically and for any indication that my heart had changed.

No sooner did Genni return home than I received a text from CJ, and we started once more. The surgery hadn't healed my heartbreak over the relationship and there always seemed to be good reason for not just the breakup, but the makeup as well. Every time we departed; I knew that it was due to the way we started. I held myself accountable as much as I did him. No more than three weeks would pass before I'd get a text or an email with his confession of love for me and new reasons to try once again. Because I had not just loved him, but felt with him a way I had with no one else, I forgave him and began again. With him, I felt as though I was home. Not at all similar to the way I felt when I moved to Ohio, but a stillness inside me that I only came to know while lying in his arms.

Meanwhile Kaelib had been testing the waters, as teens often do. On New Year's Day he was caught shoplifting and though he swore to never do it again, months later the police brought him home once more. The thieving began to grow as did my concern that there was something more than just teenage angst. He just barely passed his freshman year and finally gave in to my advice concerning his classes. He promised his struggling grades would improve the following year. With school on break for the summer, Kaelib began his first part time job. He also began to experiment with smoking pot and with it, his moodiness increased. He'd always been a happy child and I'd tell him that I hoped he would never lose sight of that emotion that often seemed to elude me. But recently, the sweet Kaelib I'd always known would fly into a fit of rage. As the behavior continued and my fears grew, I consulted with an online psychiatrist for a professional opinion.

The doctor explained that while some things could be considered typical teenage behavior and rebellion, it would be too early to tell if it was something more. He advised that his depressive

moods, followed by times of elation should be

monitored, but reassured me that in most cases, it

was nothing to be concerned about. Feeling relieved,

I agreed to watch and wait.

Then one summer afternoon, Kaelib was late coming

home from work yet again. I'd just recovered from

another laparoscopy, where my uterus was ablated

and my ovarian tubes removed, in an effort at

alleviating my pain and need for hormones. I was

still a bit tender and sore and had made it clear to

him that I would need help cleaning and was

depending on him to be home. Hours later, Kaelib

strolled in without apology. He'd grown distant, but

again I chalked it up to being a teen who had

outgrown his need for nights out with mom and

binge-watching Die Hard together. This was a rite of

passage. He should want to be with his friends more than me, I told myself.

When he appeared, I raised my voice in frustration.

"You were supposed to be home hours ago! Where have you been?" I asked.

"I was out with friends. Why are you so upset?" he asked blankly.

"I told you I needed your help today. I can't do all of this on my own."

The argument escalated, with him quickly losing his temper. He became red-faced and went into a fit of rage. He took his shoe and threw it at me, screaming now about something indecipherable.

"Kaelib! Why are you acting this way?" I demanded. His screaming continued and his anger consumed him. I was at a loss to understand and frustrated by his reaction. I began to approach him, to hug him, to calm him. He leaned in and spit in my face. He screamed that he didn't want to be here and reached for the knob, slamming the door behind him. I stood there looking around at the disheveled room. I tried to make sense of what had just occurred. I opened the door where he'd exited and looked out, but he was gone. Hours passed and he hadn't returned. I called CJ and filled him in on the event. He assured me that Kaelib was out cooling off and would return soon. He coaxed me out to meet him for dinner and comforted me while we both imagined that by the time I returned, Kaelib would be home.

I pulled up in front of the townhouse a couple hours later, but when I entered there still was no sign of Kaelib. The next morning I woke to an empty home and debated on what to do. He probably decided to stay at a friend's house, I assured myself. So I got dressed and headed to work, but after an hour I couldn't take the worry and decided to actively search for him. I drove up and down the streets and to the parks where I knew he practiced skateboarding. He hadn't reported for school and wasn't in any of the usual places. The day wore on with no sign of him. I felt lost as to what to do next. I racked my brain for the answers, but came up short. My heart filled with fear and worry. I was taken aback by the interaction that unfolded and couldn't wrap my mind around what prompted him to become so angry that he felt that the only answer was to run away.

Unlike the time in Kentucky where Kaelib took off in the middle of the night over some slight, this wasn't a small town, and he had no free rein to run the streets. Admittedly, I didn't even know he was gone that night until I heard a knock on the door and saw him through the kitchen window. A short walk around the neighborhood had cooled him down and we talked through the problem without incident.

By early evening, CJ was on the lookout for him as well. He stalked one side of town and I, the other. We met up and ventured to the high school where the Homecoming Game was taking place. We'd hoped that Kaelib had decided to join his friends there. This time I left the front door unsecured. The risk of someone robbing me blind was still far less than the thought of my son returning to a locked door.

At the football game no one had seen him. We stopped teens of all ages and teachers too. Asking if they knew his name and showing a photo of the son, I'd hope would be home soon. We left the game with no sightings. He wasn't at any of his friend's houses, and they appeared surprised that Kaelib ran away and promised to call me if he asked for safe harbor.

When we became exhausted from our worry, CJ and I parted ways to return to our respective homes. I made one last sweep just in case, while pondering where he may have gone. Although his raging fit had left me on edge and a bit frightened, it was quickly forgotten and replaced with panic and despair.

I pulled into the lot of the townhouse and walked to the front door. With my hand on the knob, I held my breath for a moment and wished that Kaelib would be on the other side. The handle turned and there, lying on the couch, was my son, asleep.

"Kaelib!" I exclaimed as I rushed over to hug him.

"Mom, I'm so sorry!" He said in a voice reminiscent of the child he once was.

"I've been so worried about you. I looked everywhere! CJ and I have been all over the place and went to your friends' houses and your school.

Where have you been?"

"I walked all over and hung out by the pool at one of the apartment complexes, and I ended up sleeping in the woods," he told me.

"Why did you do that, Kaelib?"

"I was so angry, and I don't know why. I saw my bookbag sitting outside the front door. A few hours later when I came back, you were gone. I thought that was your way of telling me you didn't want me here anymore."

"Kaelib, why would you ever think that? I love you. I put your bag by the front door because it had your key in it and I didn't want you to be locked out if you came home."

"I don't know mom. I don't know why I'm doing any of these things. I just don't know what's happening to me," he said sadly. "I was doing some research, and I think I have bipolar disorder."

I was surprised by the anger that grew inside of me. I tried to suppress the sudden rage I felt at the thought of my son being anything like my father.

"I don't think that's true. I do know that I love you and I know that there are a lot of people who care about you and love you too. Half of this town has been worried and looking for you. I don't know what you're going through, but I'm here. You can talk to me," I reassured him.

"I love you too, Mom. I'm sorry I worried everyone," he said with his arms reaching out for a hug.

I squeezed him tight and hugged him for a long time.

The next day when CJ came over, he squeezed him tight too, relieved that Kaelib had returned unharmed.

"Hey kiddo. I was so worried about you! Your mom and I looked everywhere, but I'm just glad you're okay," he said as he hugged him again.

His long arms wrapped around Kaelib and he picked him up in a bear hug as though Kaelib was a toddler. The three of us spent the day at a BBQ where I watched Kaelib play basketball and talk with the other teens. As we sat down to eat, I eyed my son, who was carelessly gorging on hamburgers and potato salad, as if nothing had ever happened.

The happy reunion didn't last long. Kaelib would alternate between almost childlike emotions and cry to me as if he were, in fact, a child. CJ revved up the amount of time spent with the teen who "just needed a little guidance," he said. He'd buy him new skateboards and take him on shopping trips or to the arcade. Once, CJ spent all evening playing any video game Kaelib had appeared interested in.

When Kaelib came home drunk in the middle of the

day, I drove him over to the shop where CJ was

working on his truck. I coaxed Kaelib out of the car

and instead of continuing his work, CJ spent the rest

of the evening teaching him how to change breaks.

Albeit a good skill, but invaluable time together. I

could see the care and concern and the special time

spent with Kaelib. It reminded me of my own

stepfather, who'd taken on two daughters that

hadn't asked to be parented by him. It is by far a

difficult job to be a parent, but a much tougher one

to be a stepparent. I quietly observed the budding

relationship with hopes that Kaelib would embrace

the love from this stranger, who wanted nothing

more than to be his friend.

When it came time, I took Kaelib to the park. We

spent many afternoons there, walking and admiring

the flowing river and flower gardens.

"CJ and I would like to get a house together," I

started. "What do you think about that?"

"I knew that it would lead to this eventually," Kaelib

said without inflection.

"How do you feel about us all living together?" I

asked him.

"Will I have to change schools?" Kaelib asked.

"No. I don't want you to have to start all over again. I

understand what that's like," I said reassuringly.

"Well okay, then."

"If you're concerned about us living together, we can

talk about it. You can tell me how you feel." I urged

him to speak his mind since it was never my

intention to have my son put my well-being before

his own. My job was to ensure that he was happy. I

made it my priority to protect his childhood. He of

course wasn't oblivious to my worries and concerns;

however, I would not allow him to bear the weight of adult responsibilities, as I knew all too well what it felt like to be a child who was burdened with concerns. I wanted him to know the joys of childhood because all too soon it would be over, leaving him challenged under the weight of the world. I acknowledged that he may not be pleased with the aspect of moving, but I wanted to allow him a choice. A courtesy my parents had never granted me.

"I think it'll be good. I've never had a stepdad before. Sure, it'll be a little weird at first since it's always been just me and you," he said with a little spark in his voice.

"It might be at first, but as long as you feel okay with it. I want you to be a part of this decision too."

"I'm okay with it, Mom. I just didn't want to change schools," he confirmed.

So, it was settled. With Kaelib coming full force into his teenage years, I felt it even more important that he have a male figure who might be able to show him ropes that I could not. Although I never doubted my abilities as a mother, surly there were things about boys who would soon grow into men, that I wouldn't know.

Months passed as we packed and prepared. Finally, the first weekend of October arrived, and I was more than happy to say goodbye to the drab townhouse. I pulled onto the street for the final time and was surprised to see a crowd of kids and what appeared to be a fist fight taking place. I couldn't quite make out who the children were, but I was no stranger to inserting myself into any perceived wrongdoing. My days as a bullied young girl had instilled in me a righteousness of sticking up for the underdog.

No sooner did I shift the car into Park, ready to jump out and break up the group, than Kaelib appeared.

His nose was bloody and the bruises had already started to form near his eyes. His short haircut was matted atop his head and there were red marks in the shape of fingerprints on his neck. I opened the car door in disbelief!

"I'm fine, Mom," he said.

"Kaelib, what in the world happened?!"

"I'm fine, Mom," he stated again as he moved to the front door with me following behind him.

"I want to know what is going on!" "I asked for it," he said smugly.

"What do you mean, you asked for it?"

"Yeah, I told Dillon that I wanted to fight him, and so when we got off the bus, we did," he explained.

"Dillon used to be your friend. Why did you want to fight him?"

"Because we're not friends anymore, and he was being a jerk!" Kaelib exclaimed.

The rush of the last couple of years and the constant battle with his moods simmered inside me. The drinking and smoking pot, the stealing and running away, the lies; all of the endless lies! I uncovered a secret fight club he'd created when I cracked the PIN on his phone one day. The bruises had tipped me off, but when I confronted him he lied and said he was injured when he was working out. He often talked about the movie *Fight Club* and it had become an unhealthy obsession, but I was still shocked to find that he interjected himself into his own manifestation.

What was I to do now? I debated pressing charges against Kaelib's former friend who had bloodied my son. I didn't know the answer, so I texted Genni. She and I had grown apart since she became pregnant again. Although the drama between CJ and me had finally evened out over the last couple years, I endured never ending turmoil where Kaelib was concerned. It overpowered any happiness I felt I earned and left little time for Genni and her new joy.

I sent a text with a picture of Kaelib's bruised and battered face. Her response was that I asked for this by leaving Kentucky and moving to the city. I reread the text from the friend I considered to be nothing less than a sister. We'd shared so much, including that special moment so many years ago, where she severed the umbilical cord that tied my son to me. I didn't respond. I couldn't find it within myself to reply to the hateful words. My emotions were muted as my mind struggled to unravel the twisted events. I couldn't understand what I'd done to deserve her response. Admittedly, I had let Genni down in this

vulnerable time in her life. But I wasn't able to pull

myself away or share in her glory, while my child

was spiraling down into darkness, and I could do

nothing to save him from himself.

The Perfect Home

CJ and I spent months searching for the perfect home for our new family. It had been a challenge. The housing market was full of renters and each time we'd arrive to view a house, we were told that it was already rented or that they received more than enough applications. I began stalking the internet and following all of the homes listed as "coming soon." I'd check their status multiple times a day. Finally, one home had just been changed to "for rent."

It was a three-bedroom ranch in a small neighborhood that was lined with homes built in the fifties. My favorite thing was the hot tub in the gazebo. For CJ, the best part was the garage, which contained a working lift. The perfect enhancement for a car enthusiast! When we opened the front door, we were nearly blinded by the stark and drab yellow walls that appeared to have been untouched for the past decade. As we made our way to the master bedroom, we determined that it would easily accommodate a queen bed. However, CJ and I immediately hated the cold blue walls and wondered if the owners would allow us to repaint them. The old wooden floors were stained from years of heavy foot traffic and grime, and as we came to the end of the hallway, I stopped to eye the last bedroom. It was the only one with two windows, and I immediately knew that it would be perfect for Kaelib. I imagined him drawing and studying in the bright room, already arranging his furniture in my mind.

Although the house was just outside of Kaelib's current school district, I agreed to drive him to and from every day. In the early mornings we'd ride along in silence, and at the end of the day we'd make the return journey while I'd probe him with questions. I asked about friends and of any girls he thought about dating. His teeth held strong as I pulled at each one, only to be met with the all-toofamiliar phrase, "fine." Everything was fine, friends were fine, life was fine, school was fine. He reported nothing new, and he asked nothing of me.

At home he'd retreat to his room and then depart shortly after with friends who would drive to the house to collect him. I knew the change was difficult but reassured him that I was still, as always, there for him. I tried to recall my own challenges as a teen and remembered wanting nothing more than to be free with my friends, where I could explore who I was and who I hoped to become. He too should have those moments, I decided. Those moments are short until the responsibilities of adulthood come knocking and that freedom is replaced with work and the intricacies of life, as well as troubles of your own.

On Saturdays he'd rarely get out of bed, and the chores would be left unattended, which grew on my already frayed nerves. I'd knock on his door and peep through to see him either drawing or with his nose in a book that told the anecdotal stories on how to manipulate people and control their minds. I thought it odd, but he often would read a plethora of materials and was interested in all kinds of knowledge. His reclusiveness prevented him from participating in family discussions, and he began making a habit out of angrily yelling in my face. CJ tried his best to assert some parental authority and advised Kaelib to stop his behavior, only for Kaelib to storm off, slamming doors and escaping out his bedroom window.

Yet there were times in between the frequent outbursts and agitative states that he was elated for no apparent reason. CJ and I believed that we must have finally gotten through to him. At times Kaelib would dance back and forth in the kitchen, seemingly happy to talk to us as he tied dish towels around the cabinet handles. We thought nothing of this silly behavior and cherished the moments of pleasantries that became few and far between. We ignorantly relished in the notion that maybe his happy disposition had returned. Just as suddenly, another incident would occur.

It didn't take a psychiatrist to know that something wasn't right. So, I found a local therapist and paid $250 to have Kaelib evaluated. After asking Kaelib a bit about why he thought he was there, the counselor asked me to wait in the lobby. An hour later Kaelib came through the door, seemingly exhilarated.

"How did it go?" I asked.

"It was great!" he said with enthusiasm.

The counselor explained to me that since he didn't accept insurance, there was no reason to assign Kaelib with any diagnosis and that no future appointments were necessary. Kaelib was simply going through an identity crisis, he said. Afterward, I told Kaelib that he must work on his studies and his attitude. I had no intention of continuing to drive him to and from school for failing grades, let alone bad behavior.

Kaelib texted the following day to say he was staying after school to work on a project. Of course, I was overjoyed to hear that he was again focused on his studies and proudly reflected on the conversations that certainly had had some effect. Perhaps it was nothing more than an identity crisis, and he was ready to return to his studies.

I arrived at school that evening to retrieve him, only to find dark windows and an empty parking lot. I called Kaelib's number, but there was no response. I texted, but there was no reply. Again and again, nothing but silence. An hour later I returned home, frantic. CJ tried to comfort my fears as my imagination ran rampant with terrifying scenarios. Finally, my phone dinged with a text.

"I'm with a girl," it read.

"Come home now," I demanded, my fear shifting to anger.

Silence.

Teens have been known to push their limits, and I've yet to meet a parent who hasn't worried at least one night about their child's whereabouts. I lay in the darkness and tossed my thoughts back and forth as I listened to the hum of CJ's snore. We hadn't had but two months in the new house to work out the kinks of life together before Kaelib began to come apart at the seams. Even in the best of circumstances, the nuances of who will do the dishes or tend to the cooking can take time before a new family is able to hit its stride and dance around one another's orbit. I was learning to balance my new role as CJ's fiancée, all while trying to prevent Kaelib from spiraling out of control. I couldn't wrap my mind around his strange behavior. It wasn't just bad choices, hostility, or sporadic spending sprees; his entire personality had changed. That realization gnawed at me. I wanted to fix it. I wanted my son back! Life sometimes doesn't provide clear answers or viable choices. So, I did the only reasonable thing I could think of. The next morning, I drove to the school and unenrolled him.

"You're not going back to this school. I'm not sure what's going on with you, but in between the drugs and running away, I don't think this is the best place for you or the best influence," I told him through gritted teeth.

We drove home without so much as a glance between us. Despite my fear mixed with anger, I tried to see through his eyes. I wanted nothing more than to understand what was happening. I wanted to convey that, above all, I loved him. I could only hope that this was the right decision. It was soon afterward that I realized that the decision I had made would be nothing compared to those I was about to.

It wasn't long before calls from the new school started and then quickly escalated. If he wasn't vandalizing the parking area with graffiti, then he skipped a class or a day. I punished Kaelib by spending hours talking with him and asking what could be changed. CJ too found himself stealing time away from work for the opportunity to bestow his own wisdom onto Kaelib, in hopes that he would find his way back. We were convinced that eventually we would get to the root of the problem. The discussions seemed beneficial, and he'd apologize sincerely for his disappointments. He'd promise that this was the last time, only for the sun to rise again and Kaelib to renege on the previous night's agreement. Month after month the cycle repeated. Like clockwork, the darkness would return and flood the house like a haywire washing machine on an overloaded spin cycle, jarring us as we clung to any sign of reprieve.

Meanwhile, I dedicated my time to making endless phone calls in order to get him an appointment with a psychiatrist. All the pediatric psychiatrists were either not taking new patients or had more than a six-month wait. How could they tell me to wait when, from one day to the next, I didn't know what would happen with my child?! It would be like telling a diabetic child to wait a month for insulin! It was unfathomable to me that I could live in the seventh largest state and be at a loss for help, in this day and age, in this country! Hospital policy stated that if he wasn't suicidal or homicidal, they wouldn't admit him. He was blatantly in danger, but without an available professional, it was up to me to help him.

Then one night, I was awakened by the recognizable bang that informed me it was the police. Two days prior, Kaelib had taken off again, and once more we filed a runaway report. The friendly officer made a house call and we chatted from the front porch. This time they brought him home after finding him asleep at the local post office. I was reprimanded by the officer and deemed a bad parent. I had no rebuttal, nor did I justify myself with a response.

What was I to say in the middle of the night? After feeding Kaelib a reheated pizza, I sent him to his room to rest.

When the sun rose, my tears streamed down onto my pillow and continued as I brushed my teeth. I began going through the motions of preparing for work and the long day filled with more calls where I'd beg for someone to help me. By midmorning, I'd finally received a return call from one of the hundreds of numbers where I'd left messages.

I was advised of two options. The first was to sign my parental rights away, which would allow the state to care for Kaelib and admit him to the hospital. I had seen how the state ran hospitals. I also knew by now how feckless they were. They certainly weren't here to do me any favors. How could I trust a state to make decisions for his care?

The fact that this was an option at all baffled me. I couldn't abandon him. He was MY son. It tore at my heart to think of how he might feel, knowing his own mother gave him away. No, not in my wildest dreams and only in the worst of my nightmares. I couldn't help but wonder about the parents who'd chosen this route. Parents who, like me, were heartbroken and parents who had no other options. I find it disheartening that more desperate parents than me have chosen it, believing that there is no other way.

The second option was to file a document with the court called an "unruly child" petition. I was told that it may benefit me, as well as Kaelib. It would not only protect me from being charged with neglect but prevent Kaelib from finding himself in legal trouble and ending up in juvenile detention. The judge would set him straight, I was told. Maybe it was sheer exhaustion or that I had tried everything else within my means, but I decided that it was time for some tough love. I filed the petition, and on the court date, Kaelib and I met with a mediator. After a tense discussion, we departed the courthouse no better off than before.

Kaelib left home again, and this time, I let him. He told me to go on without him, that I was free. I felt like he'd punched me in the gut. What did that even mean, go on without him? What I wanted was for us all to be a family. I wanted to see Kaelib thrive. I wanted him to know what a special person he was. What more could I do to convince him of my love for him?

I too had left home at a premature age, albeit under better circumstances. I considered that perhaps the answer was to allow him to live his own life. If that was what would make him happy again, then I was not going to stand in his way. Days later, he called and revealed that he hadn't been living with the friend who initially collected him and his things, but that it was a ruse. His boxes of possessions were stolen by others who pretended to be his allies. He'd been living in the woods, and with it turning cold, he wanted to return home.

No sooner did we get Kaelib settled back into his bedroom than the call I had been waiting for came through. There was an opening at the psychiatrist's office. The appointment was lengthy and thorough and included pages of paperwork and evaluations. Then after a session with me and Kaelib and finally with Kaelib alone, we sat down for a final time with the counselor. She stated Kaelib's diagnosis and talked through what it meant to have bipolar I.

Whereas bipolar II involves depressive episodes that last at least two weeks and are paired with at least one hypomanic episode, which include a persistently elevated or irritable mood, bipolar I is defined by manic episodes that last at least seven days or by manic symptoms that are so severe that a person needs immediate medical care. With bipolar I, depressive episodes occur as well and may last for up to two weeks. Unfortunately, people who suffer from bipolar I also tend to experience more severe symptoms and episodes.

This time I didn't feel angry or believe he was (or could be) anything like my father. I felt sad, horribly, and deeply sad. I couldn't help but wonder what this meant for Kaelib and his future. Next, we were informed that the wait for medication would be between six and eight months! I pondered again how that could even be possible. Adults didn't seem to have difficulty making appointments and receiving medication, but for children in need, it was a desperate waiting game.

I resumed my search. Day after day, I looked up numbers of resources and doctor's offices. I called any number I could find in search of help. I called numbers that I knew wouldn't be able to help, in hopes they knew of someone or some place that could. I called NAMI and ADAMH (alcohol, drug addiction and mental health board of Ohio) who sympathetically admitted that they were also aware of the wait time for children's psychiatric medications. Often by the end of the call, I would weep.

I was driven to the brink of my own sanity at times. A mother on the verge of losing her son and the life I dreamed for him. CJ was at a loss as well and our relationship suffered under the pressure. He did his best to console me, while his own anger over the situation bubbled over like hot molten lava. We'd threaten to leave one another in blowout arguments over absolutely nothing. When your life has been turned upside down and inside out, the wrong look or the lack of inflection in an innocent comment can be enough to start an argument.

Our pain, anger, exhaustion, and despair were balled into words and thrown at one another, making sure to create enough hurt to reflect the turbulence we held within us, until our anger fizzled like a steam engine running out of coal. Then we would collapse into tears and try again. Our relationship was as torn and tattered as an old rag and whatever strength I had left, I worked at mending it.

Support was not easy to come by and although I'd call my mother for comfort, she was not able to provide me with any wisdom. Friends could not understand my broken plans that I eventually stopped making, never knowing what each day would have in store and so, they too fell by the wayside. CJ and I resorted to attending support groups where we'd listen to many similar stories from parents with adult children suffering from the same illness or sometimes worse. Some shared stories of how their child had taken their own lives. After seeing the dads who appeared so strong, sitting across the table weeping with gut-wrenching sadness, CJ and I succumbed to the hopelessness, so we didn't return.

Life was shattering around me, but I had no time to focus on anything but saving my son! His child-like emotions tore at my heart, but when he told me he could not feel love, I felt a sadness I never felt before. It was as though my soul had left my body. I felt myself split in two and drift away as I begged the universe for mercy. There was no yoga pose or prayer that provided me clarity or comfort. I was distraught and utterly alone. Running on nothing more than adrenaline, I'd lay my head down on my desk at work and awake hours later from my cell ringing with another incident.

So when the familiar number from the school appeared on my cell, telling me that Kaelib was drunk, spitting on the floor and hitting himself in the face, I knew what had to be done. I drove to the school feeling just as helpless as I had been as a child who pined for her broken family. Like a song on repeat, I cried and vowed that I would save my baby, my son, before he too became just a memory of someone I used to know.

Throughout the many calls, I was able to find a center for days like today. Kaelib could stay for a bit while awaiting treatment and I too could have a moment to collect my emotions, which fell out of the many seams I'd sewn much too loosely. I pulled up to the large Victorian that housed the many children who were working through childhoods that made

Kaelib's problems (or even my childhood) look like

those of a charmed life. We approached the worn

stairs that were marked with sidewalk chalk from

the latest residents who, no doubt, had a

muchdeserved moment of innocence. Pink and blue

names were strewn about and scrawled just outside

the doorbell as I reached to buzz it. We were happily

greeted and shown the downstairs quarters, a living

area with a piano, a full kitchen, and an art room. I

looked at my son's face, which was mixed with

childlike features and versions of the man he was

yet to become. A stray hair protruded from his chin

and his eyes beamed with light green and gray. I

quietly bit my lip and attempted to find the right

thing to say, while searching my soul for the courage

to say them.

"Kaelib, I love you. I want you to know that. You'll stay here for a little while so I can work on getting help for you. It's going to be okay," I said to him reassuringly, as much as to myself.

I leaned in for a hug, but he turned his face away. The tears stung my eyes, and I gasped for breath as I retreated to my car. I sat there for a moment but thought it better to drive away before I changed my mind and rushed back into the Victorian, sweeping him into my arms. I knew that would be of no use. As in the years prior, I wasn't able to bring back the boy I had known.

His illness was out of my league, and it demanded that I know how stupid I was by its nonstop drilling of my heart. It knew no mercy or cared for the shambles that my life had become. It tormented me with its lies and stealing. It felt as though it mocked my attempts to help, and it devoured the person, the son, I had known. It had stolen precious time. Time

my child would not recover and relationships that

would not survive. I drove home helpless and

succumbed to the excruciating silence of his absence

in my home.

Over the next two weeks, I relentlessly called the

children's hospital and urged, begged, bargained,

and pleaded for them to admit Kaelib. Finally they

agreed. It was imperative that he receive a diagnosis

by a psychiatrist, who could provide him with the

medications that would allow him to lead the life

that he so rightfully deserved. I imagined the right

medication would propel him back to his old self

and enable him to fulfill the dreams he told me of as

a child. He'd be a physicist or a stunt man or one of

the many aspirations of which I knew he was all too

capable of.

With the hospital arranged, I drove back to the Victorian to retrieve him. He smiled as we sat on the stoop together in the afternoon sun. I had brought along a song with me. A song that I deemed his baby song and that represented our lives together, which was fading as though it were simply a single day, and now dawn was turning to night.

My mother and father had started the tradition, bestowing each child with a song that represented how they felt when we arrived into this world. After having two sons, they tried to conceive a girl, using a "recipe" they'd read about in a magazine. It was a success and April was born to the lyrics of "Isn't She Lovely," by Stevie Wonder. They couldn't have been happier than to welcome their little girl. The pregnancy in itself was a breeze, so much so that during her checkup, the doctor instructed my mother to go directly to the hospital. She was In active labor, although she had only experienced slight cramping. She brushed off the instructions and decided to stop off to meet with her bowling league and played a full set!

I, on the other hand, had been an accident. My mother had been on birth control when I was conceived. It wasn't that I hadn't been wanted, I just hadn't been planned for. It became a difficult pregnancy at seven months when my parents were returning home in the early evening and were struck by a drunk driver. My mother spent the next six weeks in a full body cast with only her growing belly protruding out like an over roasted marshmallow.

Due to the accident, my mother's labor with me was also difficult. After many excruciating hours they realized that a C-section was necessary and rushed her into surgery. I was born with the umbilical cord wrapped so tightly around my neck I was within minutes of dying. My father was the first to see me. He decided that I was so peaceful, my name would be Harmonie, much to the dismay of April, who'd decided early on that I should be called Jessica. When my parents finally brought me home, their family was complete. They agreed that they had such a "sweet life," that the song of the same name by Paul Davis was to be mine.

My pregnancy with Kaelib was difficult as well, and I would joke that because of this, he had to promise to be the best baby anyone had ever known. He'd kick my ribs or get hiccups for hours that would send my belly into fits of up-and-down movements, letting me know that he didn't agree to this arrangement. When a remake of "Just the Two of Us" debuted two years earlier, I enjoyed it but hadn't given it much thought. Early in my pregnancy,

I knew I'd receive little support from Kaelib's

biological father, and one day, while driving home

from work, the song came on the radio. I knew

instantly that it was my song for my baby. It could

not have been any closer to what I felt for him and

my aspirations for myself as a new parent.

I needed Kaelib to know so many things, to

understand. I was at a loss. So many times before I

told him how much I loved him. Yet now I knew

talking couldn't fix this, and it certainly couldn't

change his illness. I couldn't make sense of it, and he

too struggled to understand it, to understand

himself. All I could do was explain what he might

expect at the hospital and give him my

encouragement. I knew without professional help

that he might not only physically harm himself, but

that his rash decisions, fueled by his uncontrollable

emotions, paranoia, and delusions, could alter his

life forever.

I told him that this might be the last time anyone

was able to save his life. He was just four months shy

of eighteen, and the indiscretions that were often

overlooked would soon hold him to a higher

accountability. Maybe it was better that he had an

early onset. Unlike my father who had an entire

family to care for when his illness became apparent,

Kaelib was young and could get the help he needed

and lead a meaningful life. By the time we made it to

the hospital, the awkwardness had fallen away. It

almost felt as though he was going to the doctor for

some menial ailment. Then his name was called, and

he disappeared through the door.

I'd visit Kaelib after work and spend hours in the

small room with the uncomfortable brown leather

couches. At times I'd find a dancing, rapid talking

Kaelib and others he would sit across from me, stone faced and hostile, with arms crossed and a look on his face that could not be mistaken for any less than his annoyance at my presence. CJ would accompany me other times. We'd wait again on the couch and CJ would search the barren room with his eyes and listen to the announcements on the PA, unable to hide his discomfort.

During one visit, CJ brought along socks to ensure Kaelib would have plenty. When he discovered that Kaelib still hadn't received them, he demanded in person that they be given to "the young man." Through gritted teeth, he sternly informed the staff of how unacceptable it was that Kaelib be deprived of warm feet! I suspect that it was not so much the socks he cared about, but the amount of love they carried to his soon to be stepson.

Two weeks into his treatment I was informed that Kaelib was attacked by another patient. CJ and I promptly drove to the hospital and withdrew him, knowing that he was still on the verge of the medication making its presence known. Upon returning home, we filled prescriptions for his medications and each day, I'd sneak into Kaelib's room counting each pill, one by one, to settle my suspicious mind. Then Kaelib became still. His once out of place laugh was replaced with the smile that was familiar and the running and rambling speech was corrected with coherent conversations. He returned to school and transferred to the accelerated program. As a junior, he finished the almost two years of required education and officially graduated in just two weeks!

Because it was midyear, there was no grand stage in which I imagined I'd see him walk across to receive his diploma. There was no family celebration and after parties with friends. So CJ and I cooked up a plan to reward Kaelib for his hard work and his new title as a High School graduate. We rented a limo, and I purchased an official cap and gown, which I hung in his closet with a note that instructed him to write something that confessed his feelings about his momentous accomplishment.

When CJ and I arrived with the limo, Kaelib came out looking as handsome as any graduate I had ever seen. He beamed with pride at the man he was becoming, and we relished in the shift that had finally returned my son to me. We celebrated in the park with the large oaks whose leaves had turned from a lush green to the golds and oranges that announced a new season has begun. Kaelib read his graduation speech and I presented him with a necklace that contained his birthstone. There were no professional photographers or classmates. There were no friends and family. There were no others that mattered. There were just us three, smiling in the moment of pride and new hope for the future.

With high school behind him, we discussed what the road ahead might look like. The medication would be an integral part of his future success. We were all still raw from the last few years and I knew that without structure, Kaelib would falter. He was reluctant to go off to a university and I agreed that his fragile state may be a hindrance. So, I suggested an opportunity at Job Corp. He could work on a certification in the medical field or even enroll in college while living in the housing. I knew there was still work to be done where Kaelib was concerned. Having already hit so many dead ends, I knew I wouldn't be able to attend to his rebellion and his need for independence, all while distributing his medication and ultimately becoming his gatekeeper.

Who was that helping, I pondered. Job Corp would

provide him with what he needed now, at least until

he was ready to choose what his future would be.

Again, I drove him to the unknown. He beamed with

excitement and I, with anxiety. I knew in my head

that he was just shy of becoming a legal adult, but

the bittersweet feeling of finally having my son back,

mixed with allowing him to spread his wings,

swelled inside my heart. When we arrived, I hugged

him and this time he hugged me back. We knew our

love for one another wouldn't change regardless of

the miles between us, and yet this was the moment

where I knew I had to allow him to blossom. He had

to grow and find his way without me and he too

knew that it was time. I turned away as the familiar

tears began to fall. Be strong, I told myself. Be strong

because you knew this day would come. He'll be fine,

I said inside my head. But my heart was too busy

crying to agree.

With Kaelib at Job Corp, I found myself in a new

position: an empty nester. I hadn't known life as an

adult without him. All I'd known was being Kaelib's

mom. The newness was liberating, yet scary. I

researched hobbies and groups with similar

interests but wasn't quite sure what mine were any

longer. Besides, Kaelib would come home for the

weekend about once a month and always for

holidays. Then I'd redirect my attention to him again

as he delighted in telling me of the new medical

procedures he was learning and about the friends

he made while playing soccer.

I continued to secretly count the pills that brought

him back to me, as reassurance that he would stay.

During his Labor Day weekend visit and just a couple weeks before my wedding, I sat down beside him to go over the plan.

"I'm excited for you guys!" Kaelib said.

"I'm excited too! I'm sorry you won't be able to be there with us," I said.

"It's okay. One day I'm going to go there, and then I'll get to see it too. Plus, I need to stay in school. I have a lot of studying to do for my medical certification," Kaelib explained.

"I know. I just wish you were going to be there," I said with a pout.

"I will be there. I'll be on FaceTime. Plus, it's not about me. It's about you and Dad. It's kinda weird. I've never had a dad before. You guys have been through so much and I'm really happy that you managed to stay together," Kaelib said as he looked over and met my gaze.

"I'm just happy that you're doing so well. That's all I care about. I'm happy to see you happy, Kaelib." I wrapped my arms around his neck and squeezed.

"All right, so you know what to do. I'm going to call at 2:55, so don't forget! Set a timer. Set an alarm. Set ten alarms!" I told him.

"Mom, I'm not going to miss walking you down the aisle. I'll be there," he said reassuringly.

CJ and I arrived in Jamaica just three days before our wedding. After scrimping and saving, we'd chosen a week at a fabulous resort where we'd be married; followed by another week on the opposite side of the island where we could lounge together in our first days of marriage. Jamaica was always on my top five places to visit since I was a child. I was intrigued by the pictures of the white sand and the people

with their welcoming accent and friendly demeanor.

Mackinac Island did nothing to discourage this

notion. The population of Jamaicans was quite large,

and I made many fast friends while attending their

parties, where I drank and danced all night to Ska

and Reggae.

When we landed on the paradise island, I could

hardly contain my excitement! We immediately

were in disbelief at the beauty of the hibiscus

flowers and tropical trees. On the hour-long drive to

the resort, I tried to memorize the scene of

turquoise water and the goats that grazed on the

side of the road. The Caribbean sun shone through

the window, and the mountainous road before me

called out, inviting us to explore its mysteries.

The resort sprawled from ocean to mountain and

was separated by guest levels. We splurged for a

suite, which included two of our own Butlers that were reachable day or night on the designated cell phone. The days leading up to our wedding were filled with endless drinks and adventure.

First we tried SNUBA, where we would be able to explore the bottom of the ocean. By the time we reached the location, the boat had tilted one too many times on the choppy waves and CJ was struck with sea sickness. We spent the next two hours bobbing together on an inner tube until his nausea was relieved on land by ginger ale and a good night's sleep. When we weren't ordering Bob Marley's or Jamaican Smiles, we filled our bellies with various cuisine and without a doubt, the jerk chicken quickly became our favorite. Our Butlers would prepare trays of snacks with local fruit and a variety of cheeses that we'd devour after returning from another exciting adventure.

In the evening, we'd find flower laced bubble baths that we were always too hot to enjoy. The day before the wedding, we rented a secluded cabana and spent the day in the turquoise waves, playing and laughing. We lounged on the bed as the masseuse massaged away the turmoil and anguish we'd come to know in the years before. For a time we relished in our love and the precious moments we shared together. That night, we watched the colors of gold and orange, laced with reds and purples from the setting sun, dance along the waves that swam by. It was followed by a deep sleep, a sleep I had long forgotten was possible.

In the morning we sipped our coffee from the balcony that overlooked the pool below and the sliver of sea we could make out through the green tropical trees. With a call to the Butler, we were transported on a golf cart to the abutting side of the resort to enjoy a warm bathe in the salty ocean. We looked up to see grapes dangling off the vine and lazed sleepily next to one another in our final moments before we would become husband and wife.

In the afternoon I chose a dark purple for my manicure and was told that CJ didn't report for his foot massage. The staff seemed concerned. I told them he was probably napping and reassured them that there was no cause for alarm. The hours drifted by as my hair was styled with a loose braid that banded the sides of my head, accompanied by waterfall curls, that magnified my long blond hair. Then makeup was applied, and I stared at my reflection with satisfaction.

The rain had come in just as I climbed out of the chair and finished my champagne. I wandered over to the open bar next door and ordered a fruity drink. This was the last moment with myself. The last moment before I became someone's wife. I had no second thoughts, no shaky hands or cold feet. I pulled out my phone and dialed CJ. His sleepy voice confirmed my suspicion that he was indeed napping, and with that, I was ready to change into my dress.

The wedding planner had already taken CJ to the upper deck of the resort that looked out onto the ocean. So when I arrived at the suite, I slipped into the white laced gown and wriggled my way into the van that would whisk me away to my vows. I was already late for my wedding and I tried to contact Kaelib for my walk to the altar. There was no answer, other than from the roommate that assured me he'd track him down. I walked past the pool on the way to my waiting fiancé and heard whoops and yells of congratulations.

As I stood at the platform, I could see the tall Jamaican man who would officiate our union. I climbed two stairs and waited for a moment. I looked out at the sea, so beautiful and calm. The water stood still like glass under the gray sky that had kicked up the humidity after the quick rainfall. I waited there for my son to ring through on the app I so diligently added to his phone only weeks ago.

I held my bouquet of velvet purple orchids and exhaled. I handed the phone off to my wedding planner and she assured me that if it rang, she would answer in time for Kaelib to be a part of the ceremony. I looked out once more to see CJ with his back turned, the white pants and pale peach shirt he'd chosen for the ceremony draped over him, making him look as though he just stepped off a yacht.

I could hold back no longer. I pulled the front of my dress up to where my shoes would be free to climb the remaining steps and tried to run, but to my dismay, I realized that my dress hadn't been altered enough to allow such free movement. I hurriedly stepped one by one and ascended at the top of the short staircase. Then I nodded that I was ready for the music to begin.

The remake of Ed Sheeran's "Thinking Out Loud," sang by Dillon Scott began to play. CJ turned from his rest at the edge of the gazebo and rushed toward me with tears in his eyes. I waved away his kiss as a tradeoff to the one that would seal our commitment to one another. The officiant began the ceremony while CJ and I stood hand in hand. We glanced at each other as the officiant's Jamaican accent twisted our names. "AAhmonie, do you take Chrisstapha to be your . . ."

We smiled, resisting the urge to burst into laughter.

"I do," I said, with all my heart.

When it was time to read the vows, I watched CJ reach into his breast pocket to retrieve them, only to see his hand withdraw with his own. With my hands empty, I quickly scanned my memory and tried my best to recall what I'd written. I didn't completely remember, but the words I spoke are as true now as they were on that day. When I looked over, I saw my wedding planner standing there with the phone in front of her. Kaelib had made it to the proceedings. Now my heart was complete.

The video never recorded the ceremony, but I thought it apt that we had decided that the union was for the two of us and that the only person who could bring more joy to our special day was my son, who on that day became ours. We danced our first dance with Kaelib's face on the screen and we talked about Jamaica and its beauty and even more

beautiful, its people. We hung up when it was time

for pictures.

I never imagined that a photo shoot could be such

fun, but our photographer was not only talented, but

absolutely hysterical! He taught us a bit of

Patwa and some common phrases we could use on

future visits. Our unorthodox wedding photos had

us doing our version of a couple's handshake with

double butt smacks. Each photo was better than the

last. Some focused on our love for one another with

fuzzy backgrounds and our foreheads pressed

together, while others captured sheer moments of

delight. One of our favorites was when I burst into

laughter as CJ took off my garter with his teeth.

Other photos featured the reds, oranges and greens

of the foliage native to the magical land; with

bubbles enveloping us as I stared off into the

distance and CJ peered down as though the only beauty amongst the backdrop was me.

When night came and the photo shoot ended, we returned to our room. We were greeted by rose petals, gently sprawled across the bed and a towel shaped into a heart. Lights of colors bounced from wall to wall and another bubble bath had been drawn and again discarded. Instead, we spent the night dancing to the steel drum band and playing bar games with couples who were quick to congratulate us on our nuptials. We drank and danced by the ocean, our rings kissing one another well into the night. We held hands amongst the strangers who we were certain could never know a love like the one we shared.

The week at the resort was everything we could have imagined. From petting a dolphin, to ziplining over the clear blue river where we had plunged from the cliffs with unabashed freedom. When we found ourselves in the small town of Negril, we indulged in a happy quiet. The little one room cottage with an outdoor shower was more than enough for a pair of newlyweds. We'd lie on the bed and stare out through the French doors at the colors that melded into one another, distorting the line as to which was sky and which was sea. We could feel the waves that rolled under the cave that the cottage sat atop and rumbled the bed with its force.

One night, we crept down to the caves to take in the sight of the power from the ocean. We carefully climbed into one opening where we could view the water pounding into the rock. Its mist splashed back on us, and we watched in wonder under the bright full moon. Other nights we spent gorging ourselves on jerk chicken at the shack next door or guzzling Red Stripe and Appleton Rum from the rugged porch that overlooked the ocean. As we listened to the waves and the reggae playing in the distance, I didn't need to remind myself to be in this moment. I only wished for it never to end.

On our last day in Jamaica, we strolled along the two-lane road to a garden that allowed visitors to feed the hummingbirds. In many cultures hummingbirds are considered spiritual or a sign of good luck. I hadn't known this when I was a young girl, who had just wanted to do something wild and chose the animal on a whim for my first tattoo. Certain Native Americans believe that the bird is a healer of sorts and a spirit who helps those in need. It not only represents hope, but the overcoming of odds handled with courage. The small tattoo that once reminded me of my own freedom now flies aimlessly on my thigh, somewhat tattered and faded. However, it is a reminder of my own strength and the continued hope that there is happiness

waiting for me, if I choose to seek it.

The garden was filled with brilliant color and the

hums from the tiny birds as they whizzed by. CJ and I

departed on separate paths, taking in the smells of

the sweet hibiscus that swirled amongst the green

palms. In each corner was a new surprise. The buzz

of the bird's tiny wings could be heard from afar as

we held out the small red bottles of nectar. The

hummingbirds boasted blues and greens along their

small torsos and would almost float in the air as

they reached in for the sweet treat contained in the

bottle. I smiled in delight. The two weeks on the

island made me feel as though I was living in a

dream and this was the perfect way to bid farewell.

We walked back to our cottage in the sweltering

humidity and found refuge in the cool water that

sprayed out relief from its nozzle, that still to this day is a high contender for the best shower of my life!

Upon returning home we were eager to share the many stories and the bliss we felt that could only be revealed in small glimpses in the photographs we'd taken. The holidays came soon afterward, and Kaelib returned from Job Corp. This time he didn't bring along the enthusiasm he possessed on prior visits. His mood was dark and one morning while we were in the midst of brunch, the lies came spilling out. CJ was fed up with Kaelib's smugness and his inability to be honest, so he confronted him. The past returned as though it had never left. Kaelib challenged him to a fight, but the only thing thrown at one another were angry words.

With tempers flaring and me in the middle, I decided to take Kaelib to the house to retrieve his belongings. His rampant words streamed out too quickly for them to make sense, so I drove around the city in an effort to understand him and to deescalate his hostility. He demanded that I take him back to Job Corp and began violently punching himself in the face. When he admitted that he was no longer taking his medication and the excuses were thrust at me without a glove to catch his words that shot out like daggers, I parked the car. Stumbling out of the door I fell to my knees in a wail. The pain was unbearable. Kaelib had endured so much inside his depression and lost so much through the mania that drove his numerous detrimental decisions. The heartbreak reared up and stole my breath. I sobbed for him as much as for myself. His face revealed no emotion as he stood over me.

"Mom, get up," he said flatly.

I knelt on the snowy ground, my hands and knees covered in wet and cold. I couldn't feel the ice that pierced my skin. I couldn't stop my tears or calm my heaving chest. I did not know the cold or the hard ground. I no longer knew the day or the moments that led us here. My mind swirled in agony. Now eighteen, he made his choice, and in that moment, I was helpless. I was no longer able to compel him to take the medicine that might save his life. With three suicide attempts behind him, would there be more?

Growing up, my tears were often dismissed. My mom was infamous for telling me that I was a survivor, in an effort to comfort me. It didn't matter why I cried, only that I would survive it. Finally, as a young woman, I corrected her. I am not a survivor, I told her. I hadn't simply continued to exist, nor had I just survived. I am a fighter. I remembered this now as I stared down at the rocky pavement through the

haze of my tears. I dug into the depths of my soul for

the remaining tidbits of strength I had left. It was as

if a switch had been flipped. I stood up then and

wiped the snow from my pants. I turned to look at

Kaelib. There was no expression of remorse or

concern, only the red cheeks and the new bruised

eye forming from his outburst just moments before.

"Let me take you to the hospital, Kaelib. You could

get back on the medication," I pleaded.

"No. Take me back to Job Corp now," he demanded.

The long drive was quiet. I searched my mind, my

wisdom, and my love for him, for something to say

that could convey what hadn't already been said so

many times before. I tried to ask the right questions,

but his words turned into stories that followed no

theme. Abstract ideas mixed with theories that led

to nowhere and overlapped into ideologies and

grandiosity. Upon arriving at the school, I resigned myself to making sense out of any of it. He was an adult and there was nothing more I could do. My love would not change anything, as I was quite sure he could no longer feel it. With one last attempt, I hugged him.

"Take care of yourself," I told him. "I love you."
"I know, Mom," he stated, and then walked to the front door of the brick building, where I once departed with him on much different terms.

The new year began and there was nothing more from Kaelib. I seeped into sadness but tried my best to focus on my new marriage. CJ too had changed after being pushed to his breaking point. We spent more hours talking amongst ourselves at the heartbreak and challenge of the last several years, rather than the moments that had been stolen too quickly, where we were able to embrace and enjoy our new relationship status. He'd comfort me as I'd

cry, but as quickly as the tears started, they would

dry. My anger would not allow such vulnerability,

and I'd pull away from his arms in frustration. I had

to go on, I decided. My heart often disagreed, but

there was work to be done and bills to be paid. I

went through the motions of the daily tasks, looking

for a spark of joy that would allow me to recover

from the heartbreak that washed over me.

Finally I relented to my new husband's request. He

deserved some overdue happiness and potentially,

some for me as well. CJ and I walked down the isles

at the local shelter where he picked out a wrinkly

brindle puppy. Bo was a great addition to our

growing fur family. A year before I had heard a small

meow at work and called CJ to come over and

investigate. He reached under the long loading dock

to reveal a very tiny black and white kitten, not

more than two weeks old. We took turns with the

middle of the night bottle feedings until the day the

kitten was finally able to lap up enough soft food to

quiet his meows.

Not long after, I rescued a pretty gray cat that had

taken up residence at an abandoned cattle farm.

Besides, I told CJ when I called to ask him about

bringing it home, our little kitten would need an

older brother to learn how to be a cat. He reluctantly

agreed.

The two cats did little to quelch my loneliness, but

Bo had secretly tickled my heart. I hadn't had many

dogs of my own and was a bit reluctant after Mickey

bit me, leaving a permanent scar on the arc of my

cheek. We couldn't quite decide what Bo was. His

wrinkles led us to believe that we accidentally

rescued a Mastiff, but once he grew into his face, we

knew that he was without a doubt and much to our relief, a Plott Hound.

Puppyhood is not for the lazy and he kept us busy at every turn. Bo had much to say and we soon learned that we'd rescued a dog with many opinions. He brought laughter to our home that had been plagued with worry and the feeling I'd known as a child. The feeling that I couldn't quite name. As the weeks wore on and Bo learned to stay quiet in the late hours when his pack drifted off to dream, I received a call that jolted us into a nightmare.

Job Corp was on the line asking if I'd seen Kaelib. I hadn't, nor had he spoken to me since the day I returned him. My stomach churned as the worry set in, and CJ's fear came out as anger and regret. We called Kaelib's phone every few minutes and imagined him wandering the streets in the cold with nowhere to go. Why did he leave Job Corp and why wouldn't he answer his phone? I texted him

pleading for a response that he was okay, anything

to calm the fears inside the worst of my imagination.

Job Corp called again and informed us that they filed

a missing persons report. We all hoped that he

would be located soon. The hours passed by with

silence. The voice mail message repeating that the

user was unavailable, gave no reprieve to the

thoughts that ran wild inside my mind.

The phone rang again, and I jumped when I saw the

familiar name appear on the Caller ID.

"I'm sitting in the back of the police car thanks to

you! Why couldn't you just leave me alone?!" Kaelib

said in anger.

"Everyone was so worried about you. What

happened? Why did you leave?" I asked with a

breath of relief.

"I was angry and I'm sick of being there! Now I'm getting a ticket for possession and IT'S ALL YOUR FAULT! Why did you file a missing person's report? I'm a grownup now, and I can go wherever I want!" he screamed into the receiver.

"Kaelib, I'm sorry. I didn't file it, but I texted you that if you didn't respond that a missing person's report would be issued. All you had to do was say you were fine. I was worried! I didn't know where you were or if you were dead somewhere."

"I was fine," he sneered. "I've been riding the city bus to stay warm. I needed time to think," he explained.

He handed the phone off to the officer who let me know that he would return him to Job Corp. Relieved, I got dressed and prepared for work. No sooner had I started my day than another call from Job Corp came in. They expelled him and were en route to my house. I pulled into the driveway to see an older man sitting in the driver's seat of a white

van and Kaelib in the back. I hadn't had time to

grasp what had happened, let alone contemplate

what the best options were. I was angry! I was

exhausted! The roller coaster of life and emotions

flooded through me, and I grappled with the

decisions that I no longer wanted to make. Where

was the right decision? What were the right

answers? Faced again with the conundrum, I

decided to confront him.

I stepped out of the car and gave him two choices: he

could have the man who drove him to the house take

him to be evaluated at the hospital, or I could drive

him, but one way or the other, he was going to get

help! Then it would be up to the professionals to

decide if his diagnosis was a fact or a fallacy (as

Kaelib had chosen to believe). I was no doctor, and

even with all the tools available through technology,

I was at a loss where his medical needs were concerned. This time he was an adult and thankfully so. There were no long waits for medications and hospitals. Medical professionals were easy to come by for adults, and if anything, I was relieved by the fact that at least that battle was over.

Kaelib reluctantly agreed to let me drive him for an evaluation. I cautiously headed to the hospital, unable to gauge his level of paranoia, paranoia that might compel him to leap out of the car without a moment's notice. He'd never done that in the past; however, on one particular day while the three of us were out for a walk, Kaelib grew the idea in his mind that CJ and I were plotting against him. He turned off the sidewalk into the oncoming traffic on the busy four-lane road. CJ and I ran out to hold back the cars and catch up to him.

In moments like these, Kaelib found excuses for his

actions and, to him, rationalizations. He'd say the

weed he smoked days before led to his paranoia or

that he knew that the cars would stop for him, so he

wasn't concerned about abruptly crossing the street.

His explanations almost contained enough truth

that even I, at times, nearly believed them. But on

this day I chose not to engage in half-truths and

irrational commentary.

CJ met us in the lobby, and he sat alongside me as we

waited for Kaelib to be evaluated. We discussed

what the future might hold and what help we could

offer if he would be willing to accept it. When the

nurse returned, she confirmed our observations

that his rapid speech and inconsistent thought

patterns, along with his self-reported days of elation

and lack of sleep, was clearly mania. She

recommended that he go to the hospital for

treatment again. My heart sank back into the familiar depths of my stomach, but I clung to the hope that this time Kaelib would return to me and stay for good.

When Kaelib was released a couple of weeks later, he seemed better. His case worker arranged for him to live in a half-way house of sorts, since Job Corp stated that he couldn't return yet. Several weeks passed, and CJ and I did our best to give Kaelib our support once again. At the end of the month, we were faced with the decision whether to pay the small amount of rent for his portion of the house or allow him to return home. We welcomed him back with the hope that the lesson had been learned. He expressed his excitement at returning to his classes at the community college, and a month later he was overjoyed to have the opportunity to return to Job Corp.

On Mother's Day when he called, I could hear that the coldness in his voice had returned. It had only been a month since he'd left home. I pressed him on school and how his regimen was going with his medication. He assured me all was fine, but my gut told me otherwise. I had no choice but to take him at his word. Another month passed before he called again, this time with the growing hate I'd become all too familiar with. Not only had he dropped his classes, but he left Job Corp again, abandoning his medication once and for all.

That summer he asked to see me. He had lost quite a bit of weight and the dark circles under his eyes solidified my fear that he was using drugs. He again gave me reasons as to why he could not accept his diagnosis. The excuses for his actions came flooding out, and although they hinted at motivation, they still lacked the common sense that was required. As always, the blame fell on me. I had done something

or hadn't done something. It was his own stupid

decisions, he admitted. He had learned from them

and was ready and able to take on life, he boasted.

Just a week or two after my visit, he called to say

that the family that had taken him in wouldn't allow

him back inside their home.

I didn't want him to return to our house. I had had

enough of the torment and of the hate he spewed at

me like arrows that permeated inside me. CJ finally

persuaded me to allow him to return and noted that

if he deemed himself capable, that thirty days would

be more than enough time to secure a job and

obtain an apartment of his own. Lo and behold,

thirty days later, he did just that! This time there

was no talk of medication or hospitals. There was no

need to provide him with the wisdom of our

knowledge, since he believed he held all the

answers. He beamed with pride as he showed off his independence apartment.

CJ and I humored his irrational stories and weren't surprised when he suddenly quit his job for a sales job that paid by commission only. Everyone tried reasoning with him, but he again decided he knew better. After weeks without income and a conspiracy theory he developed in his mind, he quit that job too. He often talked of numbers and how he would see a particular one that would lead him in a certain direction. He latched onto a variety of religions. I participated in his quest by reading books he lent me or visiting an array of establishments that perpetuated the belief that he could be healed.

His apartment was filled with charts and schedules that raised the question of why a person would need to schedule when to use the bathroom or brush their teeth. I saw in his handwritten motivational posters that hung on the walls and the daily tasks written out by the minute that he was attempting to control his illness. Schedules were of utmost importance. We had learned this early on. I remember creating mood and sleep charts for him, based on the many articles and books I'd read. Over the course of several months, we discovered his cycle ended or began weekly. Inevitably, every Wednesday we knew that the shit would hit the fan.

As the months wore on, the TV we'd given him disappeared, as well as the bed. He said that the TV had a "blob" on it that he couldn't get rid of and that the bed made him feel as though bugs were crawling on him throughout the night. Eventually nothing was left besides a desk and sofa he'd retrieved from the nearby dumpster.

Meanwhile, I'd finally come to the difficult decision to have the total hysterectomy that I knew would come one day. The years of laparoscopies, ovarian cysts, fibroids, and endless amounts of pain that no amount of painkillers could calm had taken its toll on me. I would plan on an activity, only to be abruptly interrupted by hours and sometimes days of pain. Wrenching over in pain, I tried to endure and continue with my plans. My stubbornness became a running joke. Even Kaelib quipped that I could have had a broken leg and would still limp through the kitchen, begrudgingly asking everyone what they would like for dinner.

Although my uterus that once brought life was removed and discarded as though it was nothing more than an old purse, I hadn't been sad to be rid of the organ that caused me life-long pain. What I wasn't prepared for was how quickly my body would change or the challenging recovery. I wore the estrogen patches hidden under my clothes and grew ashamed of the blaring reminder of the once vibrant

woman I had been. New wrinkles emerged on my

cheeks and under my eyes. I was lost somewhere in

the reflection that stared back at me. *Menopause*:

that word bounced around in my mind and made me

feel as though I was no longer on the cusp of thirty-

nine, but an old woman. The hot flashes and mood

swings did little to dissuade the notion.

I ran the gambit with holistic doctors and internists

and others that pushed antidepressants to treat my

interrupted sleep and moodiness. No option is truly

better than the other. There's just no easy way to go

from having hormones to none at all. There's no

easy way to go to sleep in surgery being one person

and then awaken feeling like a different person.

Through the years I've come to understand that

finding what works for the individual is the only

answer. The wrinkles and weight and the struggle

were a thousand percent worth it, to not be in pain anymore. I remind myself of this on the days when I feel down, and the hot flashes rage, and the scale won't budge. One thing I've learned from going through "the change" is that changes are inevitable, much like wrinkles! We can fight them, we can hate them, we can try to hide them, but to truly be happy, our only choice is to accept and embrace them.

While the surgery was a success, a month later I found myself in excruciating pain, without a plausible explanation. I couldn't sit, so I stood for hours and days. Besides, what else could be done? In search of an empathetic ear, I opened my phone and went to Contacts. My mom's number hadn't shown in the "Missed Calls" since my surgery.

Through text she admitted that she could no longer get out of bed due to the exhaustion from her disease.

I pushed Call on the green button and listened as the ring tone played over and over. Finally I heard her weak voice whisper hello. It had been at least two years since I'd talked to the woman I knew as my mother. The person on the other end was not that woman. The belly laughs we shared were far in the past. I missed that over the last several years our Christmas Eve escapes had ended. It was a tradition we'd started when we lived at the house on the lake.

Bryan had come to visit, and the house was filled with noise and chatter. My mom motioned for me to follow her, and we quietly exited the door together, giggling as though we'd just gotten away with the perfect crime. We drove the snowy roads into town and found a quiet little restaurant. We were seated in the corner booth next to the window that looked out onto the parking lot that was layered in slush and magnified under the bright blue sky. Over coffee we reminisced and shared our favorite stories from the many houses. Our lunch turned to hours before we tipped the waitress and returned to the noise and children.

Every year afterward we'd sneak off again. As time wore on, we expanded our tradition. One year we attended the Trans-Siberian Orchestra. Another time it was the Nutcracker. As we watched from the pews, she confessed her childhood love of the ballet to me. Over time we became as close as a mother and daughter could be, but now the woman on the phone no longer sounded familiar. Her voice was old and frail. I slowly watched as the woman who was my confidante, my friend, and my mother dissolve into a shell of herself. It became rare to hear her laugh that once matched mine.

"Hi, hon. I'm not feeling well. Is everything okay?" she asked with a quiver in her voice.

"No, I'm not okay. I'm in a lot of pain and I don't know why. I've been to the doctor and they can't find anything. I was feeling better and now I can't hardly move without pain," I confessed.

"I don't get it! My mom had a hysterectomy, and she didn't complain and carry on like you're doing!" she said, devoid of sympathy. "I've got to go back to bed. You'll be fine. I love you, Harmonie."

"Okay, I understand. I love you too, Mom." I pushed the End Call button. I needed her to be there for me, and yet I knew that it was impossible. She was too sick, and I knew better by now than to count on the long conversations we once had or the empathy I so desperately needed.

That was the last conversation I had with my mom. It's ironic. When I was a little girl and I got upset with her, she would tell me that she loved me. No different from adulthood, I was quite a stubborn child. I remember pouting and crossing my arms

without telling her that I loved her too. She would

say that one day she wouldn't be there to say it back

to. It was a cheap way to guilt a little girl, but

nevertheless, she was right. My last words to her

were that I loved her, and I'm thankful for that.

Days later the pain suddenly subsided. Because I'd

chosen my old and trusted doctor in Kentucky to

perform my hysterectomy, I was required to make

the long drive for my follow-up appointment. After

an all-clear, I marched along through the traffic

down the familiar highway. I considered calling

David to see if he would meet me for lunch but

found myself on the exit heading north without a

second thought.

The farther I drove, the worse the weather became.

Ice and snow covered the bridges and I felt the car

slide a bit as my tires started to lose grip. An hour

later my knuckles had turned white, so I pulled off on the next exit. I sipped the steaming beverage as I sat in my car and watched the piles of snow accumulate on the road beside the station. Just as my nerves had calmed, April's name appeared on my phone. We had reconnected over the last couple of years and had just gone to dinner the night before.

"Hey, did you miss me already?" I asked with a smile.

Sobbing and inaudible words came through the receiver.

"April, what's going on?"

"David just called me. I'm on my way over, and hospice is there, and I don't know if you're home yet, but Mom hasn't woken up all day. David was crying! I've never heard him cry like that!" Her words spilled out in a rush.

"I'm on my way! I'm about an hour out, but with the snow I'm not sure how quickly I can make it." I drove as fast as I could through the ice and snow, gripping the steering wheel and praying I'd make it there in time. When I pulled into the driveway, April ran out to me.

"She's gone!" she sobbed. I was too late.
I didn't want to go in. I did not want that to be the last memory I had of my mother. After some convincing, I did. I saw her laying there, her body wrapped in blankets, eyes closed and her mouth agape. David stood in the kitchen and cried as I too, had never seen before. I hugged the body that once housed my mother. Sometimes at night, that image gets stuck in my head. I try to push it away and remember the last time I saw her alive.

I remember it was Justin's idea to get everyone together for Thanksgiving. My mom was again draped in blankets. Her blond hair had turned two shades darker, but there weren't any grays, I remember that. I watched her eat a TV dinner with the oxygen wrapped around her pudgy cheekbones that connected the hose to her nostrils. Her right hand shook while she used the left to steady it under the weight of the fork that held the gooey brown drips from the Salisbury Steak.

The last time I saw my mom, we knew she wouldn't make it to the next Thanksgiving and I purposely chose to cherry pick that moment to be the final time I would see her. When it was time for us to go, she hugged me goodbye and I secretly nuzzled my nose into her shoulder and begged my mind to remember her smell. I've always considered myself to have a great memory. When I was a young person, I could remember entire conversations and all the lyrics to every song I'd ever heard, but her smell

eludes me, just a few years later.

After her cremation, family from near and far

gathered at the park where my mother often spent

time watching the ducks waddle along the pathways

and congregate under the shade of the Bradford

Pears. The gray clouds covered the sky as we stood

in the warmth of an unusual February winter. Since

my mother was never able to choose a favorite

flower, but had a deep love for the thorny red bush

she planted so many years ago, we decided on roses.

One by one, we tossed them into the murky pond.

My mother and I always talked about the places we

wanted to go and how lucky we were to have

traveled to so many states. She and I shared the

same love of the ocean, so when I returned home, I

planned a trip to the Florida Keys. Two months later

when spring came, I wore the purple heart necklace

that contained a portion of her remains. Now I could take her everywhere I explored. She was with me always, in the necklace, as well as in my heart.

The Last House

Losing both my mom and Bryan reminded me that you never know when the last will be. The last I love you, the last smile, that last long hug. The last time you hold your child. It's strange really, you pick them up and carry them around and then one day, you put them down for the last time, not really knowing that it was the last. I try to immortalize those moments. I try not to wait to return a text from my aging aunt and to make a call to Justin, just to say I'm thinking of him. It's all too easy to let those significant seconds and the people we cherish slip by. So the new closeness that formed between David and me had not gone unappreciated.

That summer he came to visit for the first time and we welcomed him to stay. We were happy to show off the former rental that we converted to a purchase, just two years before. We showed him around the city we called home and he was eager to get out of the familiar house he once shared with my mom. He happily accompanied us to the annual food truck festival and I phoned Kaelib to invite him as well. I thought it odd that he wanted to meet at the nearby grocery store parking lot instead of his apartment complex.

Kaelib seemed confident over the last couple of months that things were going fine with the new roommate he found after being evicted. Against our better judgment, we collected his things from his apartment, and he assured us that his new living arrangement was secure. We had no other choice than to take him at his word. We stowed his boxes, and CJ and I agreed that we could do nothing more than let the chips fall where they may. The help we thought we'd provided in the past had only been repaid with resentment; and after all, he was an adult and in charge of his life and all of his decisions.

Kaelib appeared from around the corner with a smile and greeted us with hugs and an overexuberant hello. He appeared thin and revealed he was back on a schedule and was trying, yet again, to be a vegan. He found a new religion that interested him, and he was sure that the number forty-nine was leading him to the greatness he knew he was destined for. We tried our best to listen intently, but racked our brains to unravel the riddle, like subject changes and the vocabulary suspiciously placed inside sentences that muted its meaning.

Over the last several years I often thought of my father. He was well into his seventies now. I wondered how his life turned out. He was diagnosed with bipolar at fifty, and in my previous conversation with Dan, he mentioned that he sometimes saw our father in court for some misdemeanor or traffic violation. I'd always been so angry with him, that having empathy did not seem plausible. As a child, I only saw him as an abuser and a hindrance to my happiness and stability. Now, I began to see the parallel between my father and my own son.

My heart softened as I imagined his heartbreak at losing his entire family. I still couldn't justify the abuse he terrorized my mom and brothers with; however, I was able to understand the act of selfmedication with drugs and alcohol. Searching for an escape from the torment of their minds, he and Kaelib both dabbled, if not immersed

themselves, in both. I pondered if my father had an

awakening after taking the prescribed medication.

Did he realize all he had lost, and if so, did it break

his heart as much as it did mine?

During the support groups and the many counseling

sessions I attended, I learned that the illness affects

everyone differently. Although my father had an

extreme case, many people are able to live typical

lives. It was disheartening that his life had spun out

of control, and for all I'd been through with Kaelib, I

understood how the system could easily fail those

who needed help the most. I felt my anger drifting

away from me—somewhere that it could no longer

protect or hurt me. Where I once felt bitterness, a

new feeling swept through me like the wind through

the trees. I had found forgiveness.

That afternoon we gorged ourselves on a variety of fair food from vendors that lined the streets on both sides of the river. Kaelib carelessly binged his way through turkey legs, pulled pork sandwiches, and a multitude of desserts, all the while pointing out "magic" numbers. Just as it was time to go, CJ handed off several dollars to Kaelib and instructed him to grab a few waters and insisted that he return to the same spot, where we would be waiting. Five minutes passed, then ten, then fifteen. With no sign of him we split up to go search, figuring the long line must have stalled him.

We passed back by the vendors with the enticement of street tacos and sausage dogs. The sweet scent of donuts fanned out as I passed over the bridge and turned onto the next street. The lines drew out far into the road and I searched for his familiar face, but came up empty. We met back up at the spot where

David had agreed to stay and keep watch. I made

one more sweep and spotted Kaelib walking in the

field far behind the vendors and the crowds,

mouthing words to himself and smiling.

"Kaelib!!" I yelled. He turned and spotted me.

"I've been looking everywhere for you. Where did

you go?" I asked.

"I got the water, and then I was looking for you guys,"

he explained.

"Why were you looking for us way over there? We

told you to come back to the same spot. We waited

there for you," I noted.

"Oh, I was walking across the field looking for you,

and then I couldn't remember where you said you'd

be. But I was there directly, precisely, exactly," he

stated with a childlike innocence. We piled back into

the car, and Kaelib grew angry when I questioned

the drop-off location of the parking lot he requested.

Then he admitted he'd been living on the streets. He had abandoned the apartment and the "roommate" who was nothing more than a common drug dealer.

"Just come and stay with us," I offered with a sense of urgency I could not contain in my voice.

"No, just drop me off. I'll be fine, first-rate, outstanding. I can take care of myself!" he claimed.

We stopped at the gas station, and CJ and I quickly hatched a plan that we hoped would compel him to stay for the night in the house that was once his home. We convinced Kaelib that we were all too tired to turn around in the opposite direction and promised that in the new morning light we'd return him to the abandoned van he'd been holed up in for the last several weeks.

David sat in bewilderment. For most people, including family and friends, it's only a story. What most just call drama. Yet for me, his illness was allencompassing and had become so intertwined that I couldn't disconnect with it. It was almost as much a part of my life as it was a part of Kaelib. It's a story that is hard to grasp until you live it, and until now, David had not completely understood.

The next morning I called the care center and asked only for options. They chose to send out a squad car instead. I hurriedly woke Kaelib and told CJ to take him wherever he chose. I couldn't break the trust that I'd worked so hard to obtain, only to have the police haul him off to a hospital, regardless of the need for him to be there. With a quick hug they flew out the door. Hours passed by as David and I sat in the quiet living room where only a few years earlier CJ and I viewed its empty space and agreed that our new family would be happy here. Finally, the phone

rang with CJ on the other end.

"Kaelib has agreed to go to the hospital. Would you

meet us there?" he asked with resolve in his voice.

"I'll be there in ten minutes," I confirmed and clicked

off the phone.

When I arrived at the hospital, CJ stepped out of the

truck with a smile on his face. I looked at him,

confused, but was relieved that however he had

done it, he'd convinced Kaelib to get help. Kaelib

was calm. The ambush of waking him up from a

solid night's sleep had proven beneficial. CJ smiled

again and wrapped his arms around my shoulders.

He later filled me in on driving the backroads while

talking with Kaelib. CJ had been a resident of the

city for more than twenty years and knew all too

well the longest, slowest way to reach any

destination. During the drive he was somehow able to reason with Kaelib, a task that seemed impossible just the night before.

CJ's eyes filled with tears when he described the scene of the abandoned van. He had taken Kaelib to collect his things and replayed the image of the hideout where Kaelib had chosen to find refuge. An array of garbage and clothes were strewn about with a hodgepodge of blankets to warm him on cool summer nights. I was glad that I'd been spared from the memory of it because I was almost certain my heart would not be able to endure much more anguish. The sight would have likely haunted me, much like that of the last time I saw my mother.

Two days later we visited Kaelib. This hospital was unlike the others. There were no young children or criminals who were much too sick to agree to their crimes. Kaelib paced the large room with the massive windows that allowed the flood of sun to shine in. I could hear the birds chirping along the grassy pathway just outside the locked door. As we sat together, Kaelib tried to explain his theory on brain pathways. It brimmed on the edge of the genius he was, yet still fell short of making sense. He created a diagram and drew pictures to elaborate on his thought process. In the end, CJ and I disagreed with him, and he reared in anger. He demanded that it made sense and demanded that we agree. The visit ended, but I hugged him tight as he looked off into the distance with a blank stare. "I'm going to fight for you. I'm going to get my son back," I whispered in his ear. He angrily pushed me away and told us to go, and so we did.

Afterward, I received days of calls from nurses and doctors telling me of his diagnosis and prognosis. No longer did he just have bipolar I, but he also suffered with psychotic tendencies. The term swirled in my head. *Psychotic tendencies?* What did that even mean, I wondered. The only time I'd heard the phrase was in scary movies. Inevitably a madman would be wheedling knives or chainsaws as his victims screamed in horror, just moments before their demise. But this was no scary movie.

This was my son!

The nurse elaborated as she explained that during a manic episode, it was the patient's tendency to hallucinate, have delusions, and become paranoid.

The rapid speech and the confusing subject changes were also a part of it. I observed this firsthand many times over the years. Then she informed me that, due to the length of the mixed episodes of depression and mania, not only had it damaged his brain, but he also suffered from anosognosia, the inability to have insight.

Kaelib was unable to recognize his illness. It also happens to be the most common reason that people with severe mental illnesses don't take their medication. How could I help my son when he couldn't even acknowledge there was a problem? This was the worst news I could have dreamed of! By the end of the conversation the nurse left me with one last parting comment. She said that I would never see the son that I used to know. That person would not return and there was only a small possibility that every now and again I might get a glimmer of who he once had been.

I miss old phones. I miss the big handles with the little circles on the earpiece and receiver. I miss the weight in my hand as I held it and listened intently to the caller on the other end of the line. I remember, before they became obsolete, pressing the phone between my shoulder and ear and twirling the cord that connected it to the box of

numbers. I also remember trying to unravel the

heap of cord and dangling the receiver toward the

floor as I watched it spin in a circle, unwinding the

twisted mess.

I especially miss the old cell phones. The ones that

you had to open in order to answer or make a call,

or even the ones that you pushed upward to access

the keypad and down to end the call. I miss the old

phones you could slam at the end of the

conversation! Ohhhh so satisfying! There's

absolutely no satisfaction when the tip of your

finger presses the End Call button on a touch screen.

So when I ended the call with the nurse, I pointed

my index finger at the red button with the icon of an

old-fashioned phone receiver and stabbed it as hard

as I could, over and over, as I screamed at the top of

my lungs! Still not as satisfying, but it got the job done.

I believe in science. I believe that doctors are highly educated as much as I believe they've seen one too many hopeless cases. I believe that not all cases are the same, and I believed that my son would return to me! I would do anything within my power to help Kaelib. It wasn't just to bring him back for me, but because he deserved a life, not simply to live, but to achieve his dreams. Of course love alone cannot change a person, nor heal them from their wounds. We've all been marked with permanent scars, but I knew that in time those too can fade.

Kaelib had just reached the two-week mark when I received another call from the hospital. They were releasing him. Although I'd just visited a couple days prior and hadn't seen any marked improvement, I presumed that his medication must have started to work. Contrary to my assumption, the nurse

explained that there was just nothing more that

could be done, and she was sending him off by taxi.

To where was of no concern to her.

CJ and I went round on whether he should live with

us or not. Each time we allowed him to return,

Kaelib's illness would send us spiraling out of

control. The need to constantly tend to his

medications, appointments and emotions only

added to our heightened state, exhaustion and our

own bag of unresolved issues. It seemed to twist us

and tangle our words. On the surface, the arguments

likely started over silliness, but they grew louder

and more frequent. Counseling helped us work on

our communication but did not absolve us of the

cruel words we spewed out at one another or the

multiple times I threatened divorce.

We finally concluded that it was up to the two of us

to help Kaelib, and so he came home once more.

Outside of my marital problems I was happy to see

Kaelib make progress by leaps and bounds! In the

early days, he would threaten to run off again and

end his life, then fly into mania and forget the notion

altogether. This time he stayed and secured a job.

Little by little he began to break through the

anosognosia. I was thrilled that he was able to have

hindsight and that he could acknowledge the

transformation that was forming inside him with

the help of his medication and therapy.

I worked hard at releasing my resentment—of not

just Kaelib, but of CJ as well. It seemed we never had

more than a few months as a married couple before

Kaelib would need our help again. By the time I

pulled myself up and out of that feeling (the name of

which I had not yet come to know), we'd return to the roller coaster that we were all too familiar with.

Six months later, Kaelib had stayed on his medication and was making great strides. He even saved more than enough for an apartment, but with a previous eviction, finding someone to rent to him was difficult. The housing for low-income residents and those with disabilities had more than a yearlong wait. So with apprehension, I agreed to sign a lease for him with the understanding that when the short contract ended, the apartment would be all his own. Kaelib and I discussed a plan on what he should do if he felt down or considered stopping the medication. CJ and I assured him we would be there for him, and Kaelib promised to be honest, as best he could.

Kaelib and I packed up what remained in the storage shed and loaded it into the truck. His new apartment was just three miles away from the house, but on the quick drive, I gave him a word of caution.

"I'm so proud of you! I knew you could do it! I know that you can accomplish whatever your heart desires, you just have to stay on the medication."

"I know, Mom. I'm really thankful that you guys were there for me. I'm starting to see that life is better with the meds."

"We've been through a lot. All of us! It's been beyond hard, and I hope that you realize just how much I love you. By now, there should be no question. I'd do anything I can to help you and I want you to have the life you deserve. Who knows where it will take you, but I believe in you. I just need you to know one last thing. If you choose to go off your medication, I won't go through this again. I can't."

"I know. Don't worry, Mom. I'm not going to go off my meds again," he said sincerely.

The next weekend, we were shocked when COVID19 shut the world down, and I became nervous about how I might be able to be there for Kaelib from afar. We talked regularly and FaceTimed during dinners. Similar to the rest of the world, I feared contracting it and becoming too sick to be there for my family. I feared Kaelib would become sick with COVID and wouldn't be able to take the medication that had saved him.

When the weather warmed, we were able to spend time together again. Many afternoons the three of us sat in the fresh air and talked about daily life and Kaelib's goals. I was never quite able to fully put back on my mom hat, because the unlicensed counselor hat was impossible to remove. I'd check in with how his medications were going and we'd talk about the recent clarity he saw through his medicated eyes. Although he never quite stuck with calling CJ dad, for Father's Day he gifted him with a beautiful inscribed keychain that thanked him for being his father. Behind closed doors, CJ's eyes welled with tears, and he couldn't help but feel that all of the struggles we'd gone through had been worth it.

Months later we fronted the other half of the money for an older model car with low miles, that if Kaelib took care of, would be sure to last him for years to come. He was overjoyed to finally have a vehicle and we were more than thrilled to see him finally coming into his own. We encouraged his many new dreams, from rapper to producer to pod cast maker. We didn't care what he was, as long as it brought him joy.

Twenty-twenty held many heartbreaks for more families than was necessary, but our family was tranquil. Kaelib had made substantial headway at piecing his life back together; however, he still struggled with defining who he was and who the illness had made him become. The actions and decisions during his psychosis were hard for him to reconcile, as well as the stigma associated with his diagnosis.

I think back to my mother's illness and how much it changed her. I've also considered those who are affected by Alzheimer's or Parkinson's. Even during the simplest of illnesses, some of us could probably admit that we've turned into slight cry-babies when we've had a harsh cold or stomach flu. Disease can change a person and yet, people who suffer with mental illnesses are perceived very differently.

While bipolar was a part of him and inside of him, he wasn't bipolar. He *has* bipolar. Much like people who have cancer, yet we don't say they *are* cancer. We certainly don't refer to a group of patients as "the cancerous," but society finds it fitting to call those who are homeless or who appear to be unstable as "the mentally ill." The contrast between Kaelib's alter-ego during a manic episode didn't align with the person we both knew he was outside of the illness. So together, Kaelib and I came up with an idea to give his illness a name and used it as a way to differentiate what presented itself as two separate people.

Once the new vaccines became available, we rushed out to receive them with the hope that we could return to the lives we'd put on hold for more than a year. We had made it through the worst of the pandemic and decided that for Memorial Day we would invite all of our family to a gathering at our house.

The games were set up in the backyard, and a buffet of food lined the porch. I stood at the grill, turning the colorful kabobs over one by one as I talked with family and listened in on the laughter and chit-chat. I spotted Zach and Kaelib hunched over in conversation that looked as though it was becoming more of a debate. Then I noticed a look that had been seared into my memory many years ago, and it froze me in place, mid-kabob turn.

Kaelib sat with his jaw fixed, red in the face, as Zach carried on without a notion of the brewing anger inside his nephew. Later that evening I consulted Kaelib, and he assured me he was fine. I didn't overtly question his medication, so as not to offend him. After all, it had been a year and a half. True, he'd changed jobs several times recently, but his bills seemed to be in order, and there were no

blaring signs that led me to question otherwise. As

the summer stretched on, I heard less and less from

him, another of the red flags standing at attention,

one by one. By August, when he turned down an

invitation to our special spot in Santa Claus, Indiana,

I finally spilled my fears out on CJ.

It had been years since we had been to "our place."

The last time was the summer after we moved into

the perfect home. It was a wonderful trip! The three

of us took the long way on the backroads that lead to

Columbus, Indiana. We spent the day exploring the

antique shops and admiring the city's artwork. I

remember stepping into the ice cream parlor and

feeling as though my feet were in two different

centuries. Outside on the main strip were metal

statues and eclectic architecture with large stone

pillars, while inside music from the early 1900s

played. We ordered up an old-fashioned scoop of

delectable cherry and chocolate chip before

returning to the modernization of the street outside.

We continued our journey until we reached the

small town where Kaelib and I had spent summers

during his childhood. I always wanted to stay at the

hotel with the Koi pond, but my years as a single

mom only presented me with the choice of camping

and the theme park, or the hotel and a free buffet.

The theme park won out in the past, but this time

we did both!

The theme park added a new ride annually, rotating

so that one year a new ride was added to the water

park, and the next year it was added to the

amusement park. It had been so long since we'd

visited that there were two new water rides! We

arrived first thing the next morning and rushed to

the entrance. After a short wait, it was our turn on

the newest adventure. We climbed into the large raft

and began slowly moving upward as the churning of the belt creaked and groaned. When we reached the top, a cold spray of water shot out as we plummeted down and then around the loop.

Splashes of freezing water shocked our skin and hands. Our fingers curled around the handles as we tried to hold on, gasping for breath with every shiver. Moments later we slowed on the conveyor belt and crawled off the ride.

It was a hot day at the very beginning of summer, and we paused in the sun to warm ourselves. The park had just opened for the season and clearly hadn't had time to warm the water. Once we recovered from the cold shock, we chose our next rides carefully. When we had splashed and played till our hearts were content, we changed into dry clothes and made our way to the other side.

CJ watched as Kaelib and I flew on the swings that went around in a circle. It made me feel as though I was flying. Kaelib recalled his first experience with them when he was a little boy. He was scared as our turn on the ride got closer, but I assured him that he would like the ride. He refused to keep moving and the patrons behind us were growing irritated. Through his tears, I told him that if he went on the ride and it was awful, he could punch me. Archaic, I know, but he stopped crying and looked at me with a frown. As it turned out, I was never in any danger of being hit. He loved it, as I knew he would! Now it was our turn to watch as CJ played a basketball game. He came close to getting the best score but fell short of the top prize. As tradition demanded, we ended the day with a delicious frozen hot chocolate.

Now it was just CJ and me. I longed for a family vacation and promised Kaelib a mother-son trip, so

I didn't understand why he declined. He'd given work as an excuse, but he loved it here! I don't recall us ever having a bad time. As a matter of fact, it's one of the few places that I have only good memories of! Maybe it's the combination of the theme park and the nights of silence under the full moon, but few places have ever provided me with such delight and peace all at once.

We arrived at the campground with our new travel trailer we purchased the year before. It was nothing like the truck camper I lived in as a teen. It had an electric fireplace, stove, refrigerator, built-in TV, a separate bedroom with a comfy queen bed, and last, but by no means least, a full bathroom!

We set up camp, hooking up the water and electric and opening the folding chairs as we placed them under the awning. I'd never been to this side of the lake before because I had no reason to wander away from the tent community on the prior trips. It was blazing hot even by August's standards! We sat down to rest as sweat dripped from our faces and rolled along the creases in our necks. After several minutes passed, I couldn't take my growing restlessness and the heat any longer.

"I'm going to the lake for a swim. Wanna go?" I asked CJ.

It was early evening and the sun had just dipped below the green rolling hills. All summer long, the bright yellow ball had shone down, and so when we walked from the sandy shore into the fresh water, it was like immersing ourselves in a warm bath.

The lake reminded me of all the times I brought Kaelib here. It was the first place I taught him to fish, using the pole that Bryan had left behind. We never caught a thing! The bobber would duck under the surface and the line would tug. Excitedly I'd help

Kaelib reel in the fish, only for the line to go slack

and the hook would be empty. Our bait was likely

stolen by the turtles who happily swam under the

sun-kissed water and saw the midday snack twisting

and turning along in the gentle shimmers of the

small wake. The water had been crystal clear back

then and even in the depths of six feet, one could

still see their toes. I liked taking photos with the

one-time-use camera that bragged about its

waterproof feature. I'd capture Kaelib under the

surface with his face puffed up as he held his breath,

his eyes open and his illuminated hazel iris' staring

back at me.

This time, CJ and I raced along the rope that marked

the swimming area. We dipped our heads

underneath the surface where we could reach down

into the cool depths and refresh ourselves from the

long drive. When we decided that we were too

hungry to continue our romp, we returned to make a fire and roast hot dogs.

It felt weird to be there without Kaelib. Everywhere I looked there was a memory of the two of us, but I managed to find the peace I once had known while sitting under the stars. The stillness I remembered from the previous trips returned. I could hear nothing more than the subtle chirps of the crickets and every now and again a little boy's giggle, whom I could see in the distance outside his camper, on a quest to catch fireflies.

On the drive home I had plenty of time to reflect, as well as mull over Kaelib's recent behavior. Maybe it's mother's intuition, but I just couldn't shake the feeling that the illness had returned from its orphic lair. I made the decision to follow up with the nurse who oversaw the dispensing of Kaelib's medication. She confirmed that it had been nearly five months since he'd had an appointment. I let the information sit with me, pretending to know what to do. That night, CJ and I discussed our options. There simply weren't enough. Kaelib had yet to do anything reckless, although with our years of past experiences, we feared it was only a matter of time.

The next day presented an opportunity to visit Kaelib. He was working on a new idea for a podcast and explained that he was currently soundproofing his bedroom. We ventured over to the apartment and, upon entering, noticed it had been rearranged. It had been a few months since I'd last visited. The last time, his apartment was pleasantly clean and the blinds to the balcony were open, bringing with it light from the day. I remember how he proudly showed me his flourishing plant. The plant was an impulse item we grabbed on the shopping spree; we rewarded him with for doing so well. Last time when

I visited, he also scolded me for being late, and I nonchalantly searched the apartment for a sign of his medication, but came up empty.

Now, I stood in the same room and noted the closed blinds. The plant he'd taken great pride in keeping alive was somewhere in a trash bin. Mounds of dirty dishes filled the sink and kitchen countertops. There was clutter in every direction. Blankets hung along the doors to block out any noise from the podcast room that was once his bedroom. He was excited to show us all of the many purchases he'd made: a violin, a keyboard, a shiny blue trumpet, a flute, and several others. He didn't know how to play the various instruments, but I knew this behavior as a symptom of the illness. The spending sprees and the elated mood that harbored hostility just under the surface, waiting for the smallest slight to ignite his rage.

CJ and I picked a spot to sit among the many couches that Kaelib recently collected and arranged in the bedroom. I remember the same room weeks after he'd first moved in. He'd proudly shown it off to me. His bed had been made and new artwork hung neatly on the walls. His side table boasted knickknacks that he'd collected or were gifted to him throughout the years. His bookshelf was lined with a plethora of subjects from religion to music and novels that he read again and again. As an avid reader, he never seemed to squelch the need to fill himself with knowledge. This time, the room was unrecognizable and devoid of any pride.

Pieces of foam and bubble wrap were sporadically tacked to the wall in an effort to deafen any noise that might be picked up through the new mic he'd purchased. Time and time again, year after year, I watched the same or similar patterns. I was practiced at a stoic face, and so I shifted my focus to the mechanics of the beat maker. I laughed when Kaelib used it to change my voice into the highest pitch and then the lowest. He urged CJ to give it a go. Kaelib placed the headphones against CJ's ears and Kaelib performed the same trick. CJ laughed too.

We took turns listening to the music Kaelib had created. I'd been absolutely astonished when he played a track that showcased his self-taught and natural talent on the guitar. As I stood next to him, I glanced down at the papers strewn about on his desk. In plain sight were calculations on how he was becoming a millionaire. Several notes conveyed his goals and schedules, another admission that the illness had taken him yet again. He wrote that his number one goal was to move as far away from his family as possible.

CJ and I shared a knowing glance. He'd seen the

notes too but knew that addressing them would only

bring out Kaelib's hostility. As our visit was ending, I

managed to work in that I forgot to mention his

nurse had called me. I told him that I understood

that he'd switched jobs several times, and that his

schedule must have impaired his ability to attend

the appointments. Finally, I asked Kaelib if he'd like

my assistance in coordinating with his nurse to

obtain his medications.

His face turned beet red with anger as he scoffed at

me. His smile changed to a look of hostility that I

was far too familiar with. *No* was the answer. He'd do

it himself, he said firmly. I knew it wasn't true. I

knew that he wouldn't return to the medication. I

didn't need to ask him why. I already knew the

answer. The anosognosia had resumed its grip on

his reality. A week later our phone numbers were blocked from his phone.

Although I'd been down this road before, it didn't hurt or worry me any less. Perhaps Kaelib did need space from me. I did my best to be a listening ear, but if he was choosing not to have me involved in his life while he also chose to terminate his medication, maybe we were both better off without my interference.

So I busied myself and refocused my attention on mine and CJ's anniversary trip to Puerto Rico. For all CJ and I had endured, we managed to stay together. The past never seemed far behind us, but the arguing that was so frequent and almost buried us had calmed. Yet, we were not the same people. It wouldn't have been possible to go through such darkness and emerge unchanged.

The years had also aged us. The once lively

thirtysomethings we had been were only

remembered when we compared our new aches and

pains and wondered where the time had gone. We

still loved a good competition, and the new

opportunities to travel reignited our zest for life. We

thrived in the fast pace of sightseeing and activities

but learned to enjoy the stillness of being in the

moment and making time to relax. We knew our

days were numbered, and we made it a point to live

our days in the best way we could. For us, our union

was finally ours. We chose to keep moving forward,

despite the new information about Kaelib, while

bracing ourselves for another round of the coaster

ride we could not get off of.

The End

In Puerto Rico there was no talk about Kaelib. CJ and I drove through mountain towns and bathed in the river inside the rainforest. Nestled in the tall trees we listened to the coqui frogs coo to the rhythm of the stream that wound down through the high boulders. We explored the newness of the land, and it welcomed us into its fold. We were exhilarated by its beauty when we flew into Culebra on the six-seater airplane. We explored each beach, one more beautiful than the last. The turquoise ocean reminded us of the day we commenced our love, not that long ago, in Jamaica. It beckoned us into its waters as we dove down and spotted a school of squid. Pretty quickly we realized that the closer we were, the better chance we had at getting inked. We splashed our arms in a backward motion, and as we retreated thought it better to admire them from

afar.

In planning our travels, I developed a unique talent

for finding any and all things off the beaten path.

When CJ and I arrived at the small town of San

Sebastian, three hours from the city, down mountain

backroads, he looked at me, puzzled. I took his hand

as we trekked down the pathway to the rushing

water, where a secluded waterfall was waiting,

hidden in the valley of the jungle.

Travel had freed me and tasted like the dreams of

the young girl I once was. We were unapologetically

unfettered, and yet the guilt still came to me in

unexpected moments. A voice inside would remind

me that I didn't deserve to smile while my son

suffered alone or that Kaelib would have loved that

seashell, souvenir, or sunset.

I climbed the tall waterfall and stood on the slippery

ledge. As I gazed down at the cool pool that invited

me in like an old friend, I could hear CJ yelling

through the roar of the water for me to jump. I leapt.

My feet struck the water, and I allowed my body to

melt into the cold of the fresh mountain runoff. A

moment later I burst into the air with a satisfied

breath. Smiling, I looked up to see CJ standing there,

waiting his turn.

The leap or maybe the waterfall renewed me, and I

could feel myself returning. It reminded me of the

hot springs where CJ and I sat one very cold

morning, looking out at the enormous Sawtooth

mountains. Its peaks had been chiseled by millions

of years of wind and weather and appeared as

though jagged teeth waited at the tip of its base. I

rested my chin on my forearm as I looked out at the

rugged landscape. I imagined the horse-drawn

carriages pulling settlers to their little houses that they erected on the vast land. I imagined what it must have been like when there were only the mountains and sky to peer out upon. I watched the steam from the spring waft out, revealing glimpses of a wooden cabin in the distance that sat atop the frosted grass in the dawn hours of the late summer day.

Could the joy and beauty of these moments be captured so completely that I could take them with me when I'm old and have no other view aside from the end of my bed? The photographer Steve McCurry knew how to not only see it, but to convey it. He famously photographed the "Afghan Girl." Amidst a crowded refugee camp he captured the young Pakistani child with the almost glowing green eyes. It was captivating and spoke to the beauty among insidious pain and despair.

Pictures would help remind me to hold on to this moment and the feeling of freedom, mixed with the awe of its beauty, despite the chaos and torment that seemed to swirl around me. I believe beauty is everywhere if we stop and truly open our eyes. Sometimes we have to dig to find it and to be able to see it, but it's there, all around us.

When we returned home, the silence from Kaelib remained. The calm of the waterfall was replaced with a restlessness inside me that shifted between sadness and anger. It became much like Old Faithful. It would wane and steam just under the surface and then like always, return with a blast! I could no longer stand the gnawing inside me and the sleepless nights that, at times, I'd wake to myself crying out Kaelib's name. The vivid dreams would relentlessly haunt me well into the day and saturate me in turmoil.

It had become a habit for me to Google all of the questions I pondered, along with new recipes for the week and lands that intrigued me with their exotic beauty and fascinating traditions. By far, the search engine was my favorite piece of technology. I loved that knowledge was at the tips of my fingers, a far cry from the antiquated encyclopedias I consulted as a child.

I recall thumbing through the pages and reading about birds and faraway lands, with little pictures in the corner, giving some indication as to what the various subjects looked like. I was an inquisitive child and also intrigued by my mother's large vocabulary, as I listened to her adult conversations. My second favorite book was the dictionary. I'd carefully find the words with many syllables and memorize their meanings. Later, I added them to my inner catalog and crafted them into the songs that I wrote.

I searched for answers to soothe my soul many times. I searched in books and with counselors and inside myself. I searched the internet for articles and scanned through forums. Many times I'd come to the same answer: grief had many stages, and it wasn't uncommon to experience them in random order. I knew grief when Bryan died and again with my mother. This didn't feel the same. How could I grieve someone who wasn't dead? But I felt that each time the illness reared itself, that Kaelib did, in fact, die, only to be resurrected once more, over and over.

I made some adjustments to the phrase and pressed Search again. I always avoided the option to choose Google's "I Feel Lucky." What result would it give me, and did I believe I was lucky enough to receive the answer to my burning questions? I thought not! Now

a list of several new web pages appeared. As I

scrolled down I searched not just for information

but hope and acknowledgment that I wasn't alone. I

stopped mid-page when I saw a phrase I hadn't seen

before. I clicked the link and read the definition.

Ambiguous Grief: To mourn the loss of someone who

has not died or a loss that occurs without the

significant likelihood of reaching emotional closure.

The words comforted me and sunk into my bones. It

encompassed so much of the tangled emotions I felt

in the depths of my soul. The name I could not name,

that day so long ago when I sat in the kitchen with

the shotgun that had failed me. That day when I was

forced to accept life without resolution. A grief of

sorts that cannot be quantified or mastered.

I believe it to be not just ambiguous, but ubiquitous.

The grief was everywhere I'd go and deep inside me. The joyous times weren't overtly overshadowed with sadness, but the grief sat within me, waiting for me to return to it. What could I do with feelings I couldn't relieve at a tombstone or ashes that could not be ceremoniously tossed out with a formal goodbye? Was I left with nothing more than to contemplate the "could've beens" of days that cease to exist?

While having a name for the feeling provided me comfort and was a phrase that had meaning and conveyed the feeling I struggled to describe before, there was no path forward. A program hadn't been created for this type of grief, and there were no easy-to-follow steps. There was no indication of hope that a light was waiting for me in the end. It was just before the holidays, and I sat in limbo, unable to go back and unable to move ahead.

The first of December promised the year would soon

close and bring with it the newness of a fresh start

to come. The remaining thirty-one days would linger

though, and I'd revisit the past like a déjà vu from

which I couldn't flee.

Why I answered a call from a number I didn't know

escapes me, but I did. I assumed it was another

spam call with extended warranty offers or

promises of loan forgiveness. I felt a bit

cantankerous that morning and was ready to

release it onto whoever was on the other end of the

line. When I was told it was a Michigan State trooper,

I waited for the scam, until she asked if I was

Kaelib's mom.

"Yes," I stated with a slight quiver in my voice, my

bad mood quickly shifting to worry and

apprehension.

"He's been in a car wreck here and he hit pretty hard," she started to explain. My head swam as I tried to reel myself in, knowing that more information was being said, but I couldn't quite comprehend it.

"The EMT looked him over, but he ran off into the woods before I could get here. We're very concerned. We found his medical records in his car, so we're sending out the K-9 unit to find him. I'll call you when I have more information," she said before ending the call.

My heart pounded as if I had just finished the longest marathon of my life. Knowing Kaelib had blocked my number months earlier, I made calls to friends and family explaining the situation and asked them to contact me if they heard from him. I tried to call and text Kaelib from a number I knew he hadn't blocked, but there was no response. Hours later the friendly trooper called to say the search

had ended, to no avail.

"What now?" I asked, truly not able to understand if

there were choices and, if so, which would be best.

"I'm not sure. This is a bit of a different situation. He

hasn't broken any laws and it's not a crime to

disappear," she explained. Her empathy was

abundant, and she suggested that I file a missing

persons report locally.

I sat in the lobby of the police station staring at the

Christmas tree, a symbol of unity, love, and peace,

but anger boiled inside me with each twinkle of the

lights. I was angry that Kaelib quit taking his meds. I

was angry at his bipolar disorder. I was fed up with a

dysfunctional system and the people who took an

oath to do no harm, but at every turn continued to

hand him off to the streets and his own devices. It's

been said that the definition of insanity is doing the

same thing over and over but expecting a different result. Yet that's exactly what every facility, counselor, and psychiatrist had done! I was angry that there wasn't much else I could do, and more than that, I was terrified! A very kind officer assisted me in filing the report and reiterated the Michigan trooper's sentiment, adding that if they ran across him and he refused help, there wouldn't be much they could do either.

I was reminded of when Kaelib had taken off from Job Corp and the fear that came with wondering where he might be. This time he'd trudged off with only his laptop and the clothes on his back. Not long ago I randomly drove past his apartment and found that it was vacant. I suspected that he was living in his car, which was now totaled. Where would he go in the cold and snow? What could he be thinking, and why wouldn't he just call to say that he was all right?! I brooded so that I wouldn't succumb to the trepidation that manifested itself within me. It would be a week of sleepless nights and daydreams that drifted between relief and the urge to slap him before my calls finally rang through.

"Are you okay?" I asked with concern and mounds of relief.

"I don't know, Mom," he said with a childlike tone.

"My ankle is hurt. I can't trust anyone now. Not you, not the police. You never listen. The only time you've ever helped me is through coercion!"

"Kaelib, I am listening. I'm worried for you. Can I just say one thing?"

"SAY IT, THEN! YOU DON'T NEED MY PERMISSION, SO JUST SAY WHAT YOU'RE GOING TO SAY!" he yelled into the receiver.

I ignored his tone and the yelling and like so many times before, I searched my heart for the right words.

"I'm concerned about your well-being. The police said they weren't sure if you were hurt and that you hit the cement barrier head on. Now you're wondering around in the cold and I don't know what the weather is there, but we had some bad storms here and I'm just worried about you," I rambled, in hopes I made my point.

"Well, there's one thing you need to understand," he said before the line went dead.

Confused, I dialed again and heard the familiar voicemail message.

"I don't know if we were disconnected or you hung up, but I just want you to know that you *can* trust me. If you need food, I'll drop it off. No questions asked. I just want you to be safe. It's cold out here. I love you,

Kaelib." End of message.

My relief in knowing he was all right or at least as all

right as he could be, was mixed with a mounting pile

of desiderium and despair. It took turns forcing me

into a spiral of self-doubt and the name now, the

ubiquitous grief, fell upon me like an invisible force

that sat upon my chest. CJ again tried his best to

comfort my fears and concerns, as well as his own.

His anger rose at seeing his wife with redundant

tears and then he turned the blame back to Kaelib.

The "should haves" and "could haves" came racing

out of his mouth.

"He should have stayed on the medication. He

should have called us. He could have reached out for

help! It didn't have to be this way!" CJ vented with as

much exasperation as I too had felt.

That night I scurried off to bed, where I made a habit of the nightly dance called toss and turn. The vivid dreams played out in Technicolor through the night, and I awoke to the notion that I was to blame for many things. I hadn't just faltered but failed! It all came crashing down on me, the failures of the businesses I was not able to maintain. The failure that I couldn't save my broken family now as before.

I failed at saving Bryan from the tumor and sank into the sadness with realization that I had now outlived my eldest brother. I'd failed my mother, abandoning her in the last months of her life as I could no longer watch the once lively woman gasp for oxygen. Her disappointment in me was explicit when I wouldn't come back to the home she had made in Kentucky.

Was I not to blame for imagining that I could raise a child and give him a childhood I'd never known?

How could I pretend that I had the right to be happy, and at what cost to the boy whom I promised to be there for? I failed Kaelib, who wandered in the cold without a home to call his own. I hated myself for not knowing how else to help or what other choices I should have made. The guilt rose up inside me.

I knew the truth. I knew that his illness was to blame, and yet I couldn't stop my thoughts from looping in a circle, making me wonder if every choice I ever made was a mistake. Grasping at comfort, I reminded myself that he was a grown adult and chose his path. It did nothing to take away my blame, and my mind began to linger in the sorrow.

I remembered the simpler times. The small boy with so much wonder and so many more dreams. He comforted me when I closed my music business, one of many heartbreaks that resurfaced in my melancholy mood. Kaelib was always so full of

empathy, and his young words of wisdom had made

me smile from their innocence. How could the same

person become so cold and allow me to wonder and

worry, without so much as a text stating he was

alive? Better yet, how could he hang up on me when

I only wanted him to be safe.

My heart ached for him. Such a pity it was. A

moment never crossed my mind while he was

growing up that he would become such a tragedy;

locked away inside his mind, faced with life-ending

depression, mania, and psychosis that ruined the

life he worked so hard to rebuild and dissolved the

goals he strived to accomplish. I felt defeated and

allowed myself to collapse into a spiral of despair.

It wasn't like me to give up, so I closed my eyes and

tried to remember anything that would will me to go

on. Then I was reminded of a quote I'd hung on the

kitchen cabinet door so many years ago, when I closed Music Matcher. I hadn't thought of it much since then. It inspired me to release myself from my failure and to continue. I silently repeated the words in hopes that it would again.

"Far Better is it to dare mighty things, to win glorious triumphs, even though checkered by failure . . . than to rank with those poor spirits who neither enjoy nor suffer much, because they live in a gray twilight that know not victory nor defeat." —Theodore Roosevelt

I'd known victory and its joy, and I'd seen the fruits of a hard-won battle. I wouldn't let Kaelib's illness defeat me again.

The next morning the trooper was on the line again explaining that Kaelib had found his way to the bench outside the police station. He'd been taken to the hospital to have his ankle examined.

"Will the hospital do a full evaluation?" I asked with

concern.

"Since he crashed so hard, they'll want to be sure he

doesn't have a concussion, and if he begins rambling

the way he did when the officer talked with him,

they'll probably call in a psych evaluation. They're

trained to identify mental illnesses," she said

reassuringly.

Then the inevitable call came through.

"I'm sorry I hung up on you yesterday. I don't know

who to trust. What am I supposed to do when

everyone thinks there's something wrong with me?!

I have all these thoughts and feel so confused about

things. You said you'd listen, so I need you to do

that," Kaelib said with the familiar sound of tears in

his voice.

He explained his theory on what he thought was really the problem with him and noted that he'd been robbed of years of his life. The explanations ranged from him simply being immature, to losing me to CJ, to how I forced him to go to the hospital. It was as if the clarity and conversations from the last year and a half had been completely erased.

I was accustomed to sucking it up and swallowing my feelings so that I would not scare him off or shy him away from speaking to me. I didn't revisit the past or harp on him yelling at me and abruptly hanging up. I knew too well that the wrong comment or question could easily trigger him and magnify his delusions. Mostly, though, I didn't want to lose the connection before I confirmed that he was all right.

The hospital determined he'd sprained his ankle and sent him on his way, all in less than an hour. I was well aware of the lackadaisical health care in

Ohio. In addition, the pandemic had recently experienced a resurgence. The hospitals were overwhelmed with the sick, and the burnout among medical personnel was abundant, so this didn't surprise me, but still I stewed. There wasn't any concern for this man, who clearly was homeless and had been wandering the streets on foot for the last week after a car crash. Regardless of his mental status, they handed him two ibuprofen and shuffled him out the door.

It was another missed opportunity for help. Drugs and guns seem more accessible than health care nowadays. So, it's no wonder that those who suffer with mental illness find it easier to medicate themselves than rely on medical professionals to step up. It's truly astonishing the utter lack of care in health care.

"You said on your message you'd help me. So can you buy me a bus ticket?" he asked without hesitation.

I debated what the implications of yet another bailout would be. Kaelib told me once before that I've never helped him. I only tried. This was true, I admit. I did try. I tried so many times! This last time I thought I had done more than try. I didn't enable him but gave him all I knew to give. I made agreements so that he would be forced to show up for his own life, yet I stood back and allowed him to make his own mistakes. I gave him encouragement and provided guidance because, after all, one day I would no longer be here to walk the road with him. In the end, I purchased the ticket and agreed to take him the rest of the way to David's house, who reluctantly agreed to allow Kaelib to stay until he figured out his next move.

I arrived at the meetup location armed with deodorant, clean socks, a new toothbrush, and a holiday t-shirt I picked up on a whim at the local gas station. Kaelib's pants were muddy and his cheeks looked as though they were on the brink of frostbite. He wore a dark coat that appeared to be warm enough to keep away the wind and snow he'd encountered in the days leading up to the bus ride. To my surprise, neither he nor his boots looked any worse for the wear.

After a quick cleanup, Kaelib climbed into my car without affection, but he made sure to convey his gratitude. We began our journey back to where he was once happy. As the miles passed, I did my best to understand why he'd fled. I'd planned so many things to say, but he agreed with most of my points. Much of the conversation was coherent, and I chalked it up to the thirteen hours he'd spent walking to the bus station. Still, his delusions and paranoia were abundant as he threw out wild theories and accusations at me. I allowed them to bounce off and out the opened window. I didn't try to defend myself of all the wrongs he perceived I had done or the choices I'd made concerning the treatment of his illness. I was accustomed to being the villain. He had no idea of the hell I'd gone through, and even on his best days, he never cared to ask.

Kaelib told me that after the car crash he used the rest of his money to stay at various motels. He worked through the nights and most of the days making an entire album of songs on his computer. There may be nothing more infuriating than the perfection of 20/20 hindsight and having the person you care about be so ill that they're oblivious to its clarity. He didn't convey any concern when he told me of the crash. His only regrets were his books that were left behind in the vehicle.

His diploma he so proudly obtained as the first of my family to graduate with the official document was discarded when he walked away from his apartment. The trinkets I'd chosen with love for him were also left behind. The skateboard light CJ made for him by hand the very first Christmas that we were all together was gone as well. The items purchased on the shopping spree, the hand-medowns bestowed to him as nothing more than our quest to ensure that he had the comforts of home: all gone. One day, Kaelib just walked out the door of his apartment, got in his car with just a few treasured books and his computer, and started driving. Kaelib said he didn't leave them but let them go.

It wasn't the merchandise or the cost that churned my stomach and tugged on the frayed remains of my heart strings. It was that Kaelib didn't associate what he left behind with any value or meaning. It was the anguish I felt in knowing that the items he once cherished no longer mattered. They hadn't been let go of, yet likely tossed into the nearby dumpster as nothing more than trash. Items he would never be able to replace. It hurt me for him, or at least the Kaelib I knew who drowned deep inside of his illness.

That Kaelib wouldn't have chosen this. He wouldn't have chosen to "let go" of his departed uncle's paintings and letters. He wouldn't have chosen to discard the birthday cards he received as a child and revisited each year on his special day that brought him joy in knowing he was loved. I couldn't fix this. I could only allow the pain to wash over me and

engulf me in its familiar agony.

Six years ago I made the same drive after concluding

that the best thing was to allow Kaelib to spend

Christmas with his grandparents, in order for the

family of three to regroup and decompress. I don't

remember the drive, just Kaelib's pale face and the

deafening silence. He'd drift off for a moment and

awaken with stomach pangs. I chalked it up to stress

and anxiety. I stopped off on one of my favorite exits

and pulled into the fast-food restaurant for lunch.

While I sat across from him, he slowly bit into his

burger, but retreated to the bathroom. The miles

passed like seconds, and I was so lost in thought that

when I arrived, I couldn't remember how I had

gotten there. Here I was again, driving the same

roads on the way to the same destination. Although

this time the drive wasn't silent, and he didn't just

down an entire bottle of aspirin.

When we arrived at David's, I gave Kaelib a hug as

we stood in the kitchen of what used to be my

parents' house. The furniture that once filled the

living room had been replaced with a simple

recliner and end table. The pictures of my mom that,

Zach, David, and I had hung on the refrigerator door

after she died were absent. The large dining room

table was long gone, since there wasn't a need for

the many chairs that once were the beacon of our

family. The house was almost unrecognizable and

eerily unfamiliar.

David stood alongside me as he quietly watched the

interaction. I hugged Kaelib as though my arms

could pour my love into him. I'd hoped his heart

would hear mine beating, and they would meld into

one another. I hugged him so that he would know that I was always with him.

"Remember, when you look up in the sky and see all those stars, that's how much I love you!" I said.

"I will, Mom. I love you too," he said as he wrapped his arms around me.

Now came the time. For what exactly, I couldn't be quite sure. Rock bottoms and final straws are starkly different for everyone, so was this mine? I considered all the choices I had made. The good and bad and all the grays, which I believe make up 80 percent of our decisions. I knew that this time must be different. Not because Kaelib would choose his sanity or that I might heal from the ambiguous grief I'd come to know but had yet to understand.

Two thousand, two hundred and twenty days ago, I moved into the last house. It began my tipping point, although I didn't know it then. The tests and triumphs, the successes and failures that painted my life with colorful stories and cautionary tales held the lessons I couldn't easily ignore. The landscape of my life was changed forever. Just like in the far corner of the backyard where the blooms of the peach tree once ignited sweet nectar into the air, it became sick, and we were forced to chop it down, replacing it with a new sapling. Some things can never be what they once were, but given the chance, something new and different might blossom if we allow it to take root and grow.

That night I spent hours with Zach's baby boy. As I held my newborn nephew, I memorized his features, his little nose and tiny toes. He rested in my arms as I bounced and swayed. Almost twentythree years ago I'd done the same thing. I held my baby boy for the first time, so small and full of promise, potential, and hope. His small hand fit in mine like a tiny drop of dew on a million blades of grass, and I marveled at this creation that, for a moment, was mine and only mine. Kaelib was my biggest joy and my greatest love. Might my biggest fault have been loving too fiercely for too long? It didn't come with a warning, so I hadn't seen the harm.

Pretty quickly Kaelib departed Kentucky. Over the next year he'd call from time to time, and I'd ask him where he'd gone. Somewhere far from where we had begun, far from who he had been. Sometimes, when I drove through the familiar city streets, I'd slow down when I saw a man who at first glance resembled him. I'd crane my neck and look to see if it was Kaelib who stood on the street corner asking for a handout.

Then one early evening as I sat under the shelter of the backyard gazebo, I listened to the delusions and accusations dance out of his voice and the mania

play out again like a broken record. The rain began

to pepper the roof and splash into the pond with the

golden fish, yet all around me the sun shone down

as though the cloud knew what was about to be said.

"You're barely my mother! You never loved me.

Whatever love you gave me was feigned through an

evolutionary chemical explosion that's distorted by

your perceptual lens," Kaelib sneered into the

receiver.

This time it was me who hung up, no longer able to

withstand the hatred blows. I didn't cry or plead yet

again with a God I could no longer believe in. I knew

there was only one answer to squelch the tangled

moments that had consumed me. The only choice I

had left to heal the heart that could never be pieced

back together, because it would always be scattered

inside those I loved. The voice on the other end of

the line was the only thing left that I recognized of the man I once called my son. Any hope that Kaelib would return to me once more, faded as quickly as the brief downpour. The boy with the happy disposition that I loved more than all the stars in the sky was never coming back.

 The struggles are not guaranteed to make you stronger, but the choice was mine to unravel or to stand. The life I had created and the one left in my past could no longer coexist. I had to let go of the expectation and the notion that my dreams for Kaelib could walk the same path with the man he chose to be. Each of us is entitled to craft the road before us in whichever form we see fit. That, in part, creates the person we become and enables us to find the person we're meant to be, if we choose to accept it. I had to accept this truth, my truth, and I knew that I had to let him go.

The weight that tethered me to the endless

ambiguous grief lifted like a thick fog, breaking

apart in the rays of the sun. But not all days are

created equal. While some are laced in glorious

moments and stunning skyscapes that paint the

shadows of the city as though it were an

everchanging canvas, and I find it easy to go about

my business without a second thought; others

demand that I return to old memories and what-ifs.

The regrets force their way to the surface and I find

myself mulling over the past as though it was a

scratched record, and my mind is a needle that

continues to play the same song. I've never known

what *would* happen, only what *could*. The possibility

of the bad and the hopes of the good. I can say with

certainty that happiness is not a choice, but rather

an emotion that is learned and I am still learning.

Life is not just the love you create or the heartache that follows, but the cultivated memories we lock in our mind. The fraction of moments we cannot remember and the large ones we can never forget that continue to contour and shape the beings we become. The memories that prevent us from making the same mistakes, those we choose not to revisit, and those that we cherish and hold close in our hearts. The bittersweet of it all is that they never leave us, and the one thing, the only thing, that we carry with us to the end.

Afterword

It was a bright spring morning as I sat in the dingy garage. My eyes bore into the pile of blue and white checkered bags as I considered their contents. This wasn't what I had planned for the seemingly cheery Sunday morning, but I knew it had to be done sooner rather than later. I felt my curiosity grow as I carefully unzipped the first bag. I parted its seams and peeked in to find a tattered green notebook. I grabbed it and flipped it open. As I examined each page, my eyes filled with tears. Finally, I read the last entry:

When you leave, don't forget to say, "I love you."

I am here in your heart and mind always, whenever you need, just think of me.

I can't always say the things to make it all alright, but I can always think of something we can both hold on to.

Just dream a dream where it all makes sense and all will be how it is, but with a little more calm in it.

Spring'll be coming round again and we'll all forget the grief we've been carryin'.

Don't shoulder all your worries as if they're only yours to hold.

Cause though they might seem so, they're only love turned cold.

When you leave, don't forget to say, "I love you."

And it ain't just only those words that mean what they do.

A screamed curse and a slammed door just means, I'm too upset to let this slide through.

And a silent exit doesn't always mean I'm done putting up with everything you do.

All's they mean is that this chapter's name's DepartU.

What's left is anybody's guess.

Just another mess in this home of mind I'm blessed.

But I won't curse myself to hold what's better left to rest, and neither should you for me.

Funny way of saying it, but I liked all our good times as much as you.

~Kaelib Field

Grief—whether it is ambiguous, acute, or complicated—isn't an isolated event. Each of us has been or will be affected by it, whether it's a beloved pet that we're forced to give up, the loss of a loved one, or a romantic breakup. When you lose someone you love, there will always be grief and the sun will still rise regardless, whether we choose to stand in its light or close the curtains and sulk in the dark.

It's strange how death can bring people back into our lives. Maybe it's purely the simple realization that life is short. I hadn't realized how much I'd missed Genni's hugs until she wrapped her arms around my neck the night before the celebration of life. We had made amends during the midst of the pandemic. We both admitted that we had challenges in our lives that made our long-distance friendship seem as though we weren't just hundreds of miles away from each other, but worlds away. We continued to talk sporadically for a few months, but we never could quite get back into the rhythm of our old friendship. Her life had changed substantially, and mine was…well, it was a kaleidoscope of ever-changing landscapes. But when I texted her nothing more than the obituary, she called. I had never needed to talk to her more than in that moment.

"Whatever date you choose, I'll be there!" she told me without hesitation when I explained my plans.

"I agapē you."

"I agapē you too," I said, before ending the conversation.

During the celebration of life, we sat next to each other in silence as we watched the home movies that I finally got around to transferring to digital. The videos played a much younger version of ourselves, dancing around and playing with Kaelib. He was the center of our lives and our hearts. It made me wonder if she loved Kaelib almost as much as I did.

I can't help but think of the song "The Dance" by Garth Brooks. Would I have done it all again, knowing now how it ends? Yes! The experiences of life and those who touch our hearts are worth taking the chance, knowing that we may have to grieve them in the future. Not only would I not change all the time that Genni and I spent together, but I would do it a million times over. She taught me so much about being me. I sometimes reflect on what it was like being a new mom, and I think about how Genni shared in celebrations and milestones, but mostly I think of how she was there for the

mundane. She showed me love in a variety of ways,

but mostly through the way she showed Kaelib love.

We were just two strangers that she chose to know,

and that in itself is what made her such a beautiful

part of my life.

I was wrong, though; memories aren't the only thing

we have in the end. Love is. Despite the misery of

grief and the many tumultuous years with Kaelib, I

wouldn't trade them if it meant not having those

precious and treasured moments too. At the risk of

sounding too cliché, there's no greater gift or joy

than that of a child. Kaelib was a love unlike any

other I have or will ever know. I would relive all my

pain, even if I knew that I wouldn't be able to save

him, just to relive those good years. I would go

through the chaos and the tears and the smiles and

the hugs. I would do it all again, but maybe that's

just the mom in me. Maybe that's really what love is.

My biggest fear in life came true when Kaelib died,

and while I hemmed and hawed over publishing this

book, I heard Kaelib's voice telling me not to be

afraid. Many will say that suicide is wrong and

blame those who seek it. Kaelib was a strong young

man whose only fault was not knowing how to

navigate an illness that he had no map for. In my

sorrow, I put the finishing touches on this book

because I wrote it for many reasons. I wrote it

because for so long I was afraid to talk about my

son's illness and the detriment it had caused to my

life. I was apprehensive to tell others about the grief

I experienced while he was alive because I felt as

though no one would understand. I wrote this in

hopes that someone would read it and know that

they are not alone. I wrote it because we *must*

change our understanding of mental illness.

My experiences with ambiguous loss and having

loved ones with mental illness may be unique or

highly relatable, but I should note that not everyone

with a mental illness will act similarly. Some will

take medications and go on to have productive lives,

while others will self-medicate through various

means, become homeless, and struggle every day.

Sadly, some will choose to look for a way to end their

suffering.

There is something we can do! We can help by

funding studies to better understand mental illness;

and with better understanding comes better

treatments. We can band together and demand

more from our healthcare system that should be

focused on protecting the fragile lives of people who

suffer with bipolar disorder and schizophrenia. It's

worth mentioning that there are many caring

doctors, outreach programs, and resources (that I've

listed below) available if you or someone you know

is in need of them. You are not alone, and there is a

community waiting to help you through it.

The Facts, according to NAMI (as of April 2023):
10 million Americans are living with a serious

mental illness, such as schizophrenia or bipolar

disorder.

Suicide is the second leading cause of death in

people aged 10 to 14 and the third leading cause in

people aged 15 to 24.

79% of suicides are men.

The average time between the onset of symptoms

due to a mental illness and treatment is 11 years.

Depression is the #1 most diagnosed mental illness.

People with depression have a 40% higher risk of developing cardiovascular disease.

19.4 million U.S. citizens with a mental illness also experience a substance abuse disorder.

160 million people live in a mental health professional _shortage_ area.

8.4 million people in the U.S. provide care to an adult with a mental illness and spend an average of 32 hours a week providing unpaid care.

21% of people who are homeless have a serious mental illness.

Among people in the U.S. age 18-44, psychosis accounts for nearly 600,000 hospitalizations a year.

Across the U.S. economy, serious mental illness causes $193.2 billion in lost earnings each year.

2 in 5 people who are incarcerated have a history of mental illness (37% in state and federal prisons and 47% held in local jails).

70% of youth in the juvenile justice system have a mental health condition.

Nearly 3 in 5 people with a mental illness don't receive mental health treatment while incarcerated in state and federal prisons.

Resources:

www.Ambiguousloss.com

www.whatsyourgrief.com

NAMI: 1-800-950-6264 or www.nami.org

NAMI can also assist you with an IEP (Individualized Education Program). This is a special program, also referred to as a crisis plan, for school-age children with severe illnesses or disabilities.

National Suicide Hotline: Dial 988 or

www.988lifeline.org

SAMHSA: 1-800-622-HELP or www.samhsa.gov

If you or a loved one are experiencing a mental health crisis, call 9-1 -1 and ask for a CRT (crisis response team) or CIT (crisis intervention team) officer. These officials are specially trained to understand a mental illness crisis and will know how to assist you.

Visit www.KaelibFieldFoundation.org for more resources and to find out what you can do to help, because Kids Can't Wait!

A portion of this book's proceeds go directly to the foundation for research and suicide prevention.

www.ingramcontent.com/pod-product-compliance
Lightning Source LLC
Chambersburg PA
CBHW070846160726
48004CB00003B/946